Magic of the
PHARAOHS

Magic of the
PHARAOHS

Anne Christie

D&S
BOOKS

© 2007 D&S Books Ltd

D&S Books Ltd
Kerswell,
Parkham Ash, Bideford
Devon, England
EX39 5PR

e-mail us at:-
enquiries@dsbooks.fsnet.co.uk

This edition printed 2007

ISBN 13 – 978-1-903327-47-0

Book Code: DS0157. Magic of the Pharaohs

Material from this book previously appeared in Ancient Egyptian magic.

Creative Director: Sarah King
Project editor: Claire Bone
Designer: Debbie Fisher & Co

Fonts: Opima and Alberta

Printed in Thailand

1 3 5 7 9 10 8 6 4 2

Contents

Introduction

Magic has exercised an important influence upon humankind throughout the ages. It has been called a 'pretended art', an art that can somehow influence the course of events and produce amazing physical phenomena. The art of magic is supposed to work by using its power to compel supernatural beings to intervene in everyday events or to call up occult forces of nature.

In ancient Egypt, each of the tribes that dwelled in the Nile valley had its own divinities, often in the forms of animals or birds that had been specifically chosen for their usefulness to the tribe. These gods and goddesses of early Egypt frequently appeared in more than one guise and were active in several different spheres of life. Many legends grew up about each deity and the places where their cults were practised. The deities and their legends became assimilated into the mainstream of Egyptian mythology, and some may be familiar to us today, although many are not.

Some of the stories of magic in this book are amongst the oldest tales in the world. Most of them are timeless – they never grow old. Their charm lies in their distance and age, echoing as they do, from an incredibly far-off past, tantalisingly bright glimpses of that long-lost world that was once the mysterious civilisation of ancient Egypt.

Divination and power

Divination – foretelling the future – has been practised since the time of primitive humankind, being performed in various forms, using both natural and artificial means. The ancient Egyptians were familiar with the various rites associated with the use of magic for divinatory purposes that were performed by priest-magicians.

A hieroglyphic carving depicting the sky god Horus as a falcon.

Belief in magic has its roots in fear: humans have always dreaded the unknown. Throughout the ages, magic and religion have been associated with one another, either forming an integral part of the beliefs of a country like Egypt or being used in conjunction with them. In ancient times, Egyptian priest-magicians worked on the fears and imagination of ordinary people by claiming to be able to control the powers of unseen deities. Ignorance, or limitation of knowledge, and fear of the unknown future, with its instinct of mystery, have always been common among both civilised and uncivilised communities, and those who were the most intelligent in any community quickly recognised that they could easily turn a belief in the mysterious to their own advantage.

It has been argued that, historically, the community, rather than the individual, was so certain of the permanent, unfailing help of its particular deity that wherever personal concerns were involved, ancient humans always turned to magical superstitions for help. As individuals, humans had no right to attempt to forge a private relationship with supernatural powers and ask for assistance on their own behalf, perhaps at the expense of their community.

Magic has traditionally always had the power to work wonders, both directly and from a distance, and the practice of magic has always involved specific rites. Most highly intelligent and rational people do not today generally believe that magical rites, incantations and ceremonies really produce any specific effects, however. Indeed, magical rites, whether they form part of an organised cult or not, are often regarded as being illicit. Intellectuals are more likely to see the intervention of a power greater than that of humankind and to believe in God above all else. Yet many ignorant people clung to their superstitions for centuries, firmly believing in the existence of magical powers.

Priests were the interpreters of the will of the gods.

The probability is that professional magicians or priests were originally people who had benefited by birth, study and practice from the collected wisdom of their community. Both magicians and priests acquired powerful influences over their fellows by apparently obtaining the favour of deities who were believed to control, or influence, the affairs of ordinary people. The union of priest-magician was certainly true in ancient Egypt and was vital as a fundamental power that could compel the highest gods to bestow favours through the use of sacrifices, rites, chants and prayers. The association of those who had been initiated into sacred and magical mysteries certainly had an important influence upon the affairs of state.

The practice of magic

It is believed that magic may have been the primary form of religion in ancient Egypt and, indeed, that it has always existed among people throughout the ages. Perhaps faith in magic is even older than a belief in spirits. It has been suggested that the entire doctrine of magic has always been an essential element of religious faith and that it is still closely bound to it. This may have something to do with the emotional

Carving of Horus.

response of humans to their environment and the way in which they interpret the 'personality' of the objects chosen as important symbols. Humans have certainly invested much in the belief that the symbols of both magic and religion are important and powerful.

The practice of magic has traditionally always involved interference with the forces of nature. The magician first has to appeal to a deity and attempt propitiation, using offerings, prayers and perfumes, which, it is believed, will assure success. Then the aid of the supernatural powers, good or evil, is summoned.

Ancient Egyptian magic

The stories of ancient Egypt, which are particularly associated with magic, represent the written literature of more than two thousand years. Indeed, they stretch back over four thousand years if we accept that the stories of the gods were first handed down by word of mouth from the time of the first pharaohs. Some of these stories have been collected and are retold here in an attempt to recapture their unique charm – that of distance and age.

Prayers for each sign of the Egyptian zodiac provide a basic framework for the practical interpretation of ancient magic. Sending out personal thoughts into the universe to make a connection with the one energy source, whatever form you believe it may take, is often a useful exercise that can have great value. Similarly, the use of hieroglyphic magic, with its spiritual meanings of blessings of the afterlife, is a way of harnessing this ancient energy using sacred symbols to trigger an inner power.

The ancient Egyptians believed that words contained enormous magical power. The immortality of the dead, for instance, was ensured by preserving a name, both by engraving tombs and using spoken rituals, while amulets of precious stones were inscribed with words of power before being placed on the bodies of the departed. Erasing a name was believed to destroy the soul.

Hieroglyphs, which were created by the ancient Egyptians to preserve their words, form one of the most beautiful scripts ever invented. Known as 'words of the gods', the magical and spiritual meanings of hieroglyphs were blessings conferred on rich and poor alike, promising the release of great energy whenever they were spoken or written.

Hieroglyphs themselves were believed to contain magical properties.

Ra the sun god on the right,
with Amun on the left.

The Ankh or Key was the symbol of eternal life in ancient Egypt. It represents all that is enduring and of great worth.

These ancient signs and symbols, together with the religious and magical rituals of one of the ancient world's most fascinating civilisations, are discussed and explained in the chapters which follow.

This book is all about the important influence of magic in ancient Egypt. Fear of the unknown has always been associated with magic and religion, and fuelled the beliefs in the legends which were woven into the mainstream of Egyptian mythology. Stories about ancient gods and the methods of the ancient practices of divination practised by the Egyptian priest magicians have always involved the forces of nature – the natural energies of magic.

Ritual prayers and the importance of ensuring immortality for the dead were the practical interpretation of magical powers in ancient Egypt.

Egyptian magic and mythology were rooted in the complete reliance of the Egyptians on the sun and on the waters of the River Nile. Its stories and legends are still alive. Its practice expresses the spirit and not the letter of the ancient Egyptian culture, and is relevant for us in the 21st century.

When reading about the magic of the ancient Egyptians, trust yourself and your instincts. The real power of magic lies in you. You can use it to achieve your own unique destiny.

PART ONE

The background and history of ancient Egypt

We know that ancient Egypt was a land of magic and mystery. It was fascinating, hard to understand and quite different from any other civilisation, before or since. Egypt was the most self-contained of all the countries of the ancient world, living its own life, practising its own religion, making up its own stories and being scarcely influenced by other cultures.

In about 500 BC, when the ancient Egyptian civilisation was drawing towards the end of its three thousand years of existence, the ancient Greeks discovered the mysterious and magical land of Egypt. Herodotus, the first Greek historian (whose work still survives), visited Egypt in around 450 BC and discovered that the carvings on monuments that had been written in ancient hieroglyphs since the time of the first historical pharaoh, Menes, in about 3200 BC, had survived, although they could still be read only by priests. People were still telling the myths and

A tomb entrance carved with inscriptions and symbols.

A tomb entrance carved with inscriptions and symbols.

A carving from Esna Temple.

stories that had been handed down through many of the thirty centuries of ancient Egypt's existence, and most of these tales had hardly changed.

After the death of Herodotus, ancient Egypt was preserved by its Greek conquerors Alexander the Great and the descendants of his general, Ptolemy. Under Roman rule, the ancient Egyptian civilisation began to fade away, however, until Arab invaders finally stamped it out between AD 639 and 646.

Ancient Egypt has been rediscovered over the past two hundred years. Its ancient language has been translated and its hieroglyphs have been reinterpreted, while its pyramids, temples and tombs have been excavated and carefully preserved.

Stories of ancient Egyptian magic

The magic of ancient Egypt is contained in over two thousand years of written literature and probably stretches back for almost five thousand years. In the beginning, during the days of the first pharaohs, tales of the gods were handed down by word of mouth. Later, Pharaoh Zoser and his successors started to carve their stories in hieroglyphs on the walls of temples and tomb chambers.

These stories of magic are among the oldest tales in the world. Most of them are timeless – they never grow old. Their charm lies in their distance and age, echoing as they do from an incredibly remote past tantalisingly bright with glimpses of that long-lost world that was once the mysterious civilisation of ancient Egypt.

Tales were carved in hieroglyphs by Zoser and his successors.

What is magic?

"Shew me the secrets of the magical art and sciences and the sacred operation of hidden mysteries."

From a fifteenth-century manuscript.

The dictionary provides us with many definitions of the word 'magic', most of which can be associated with ancient Egyptian magic, as well as with the practice of magic in the twenty-first century. In any language, culture or time, magic has a surprising variety of associations, including the following.

Magic

Black art; enchantment; necromancy; occultism; sorcery; sortilege; spell; theurgy; witchcraft; wizardry; conjuring; hocus-pocus; illusion; jiggery-pokery; jugglery; legerdemain; prestidigitation; sleight of hand; trickery; allurement; charm; enchantment; fascination; glamour; magnetism; power.

Magical

Bewitching; charismatic; charming; enchanting; entrancing; fascinating; magnetic; marvellous; miraculous; sorcerous; spellbinding.

Magician

Archimage; conjurer; enchanter; enchantress; illusionist; necromancer; sorcerer; thaumaturge; theurgist; warlock; witch; wizard; genius; marvel; miracle-worker; spellbinder; virtuoso; wizard; wonder-worker.

It is almost impossible to isolate a single image or association to pin down what we mean by 'magic', for each conjures up its own ideas and energies.

People sometimes confuse 'magic' and 'divination', but although they are closely associated, their objectives are quite different: while the magician's aim is to harness the natural laws and forces of the universe to promote his or her own ends, the clairvoyant or diviner simply wishes to see into the past or future. Divination, which is not an exact science and is unlikely to cause any harm, should therefore not be confused with witchcraft or black magic.

THE RIVER NILE AND THE SUN:
The river Nile and the sun constitute the roots of ancient Egyptian mythology and magic

CREATION MYTHS:
The Old Kingdom, when the tribes of ancient Egypt were first unified
The important religious centres of the ancient Egyptian civilisation were Heliopolis, Memphis and Hermopolis
The first time
The golden age
The new kingdom

THE CULT OF THE SUN:
The cult of the sun developed during the Old Kingdom, with Ra being worshipped as the sun god

DEITIES:
Osiris - Isis - Horus - Thoth - Seth - Ma'at

AFTERLIFE:
Death

MAGIC:
The power of words

HIEROGLYPHIC MAGIC:
The Egyptian oracle
Consulting the oracle

ORACLE CARDS:
The ankh - Wedja - Seneb - Boat - Scarab - Nefer
Tet - Pillow - Heart - The eye of Horus - Menat
Vulture - Collar of Gold - Ladder - Shen

The history of ancient Egypt is based on the religion and culture of a people who believed that magical practices were a normal part of everyday life. Their stories and myths have been handed down over thousands of years, and some of the techniques used by the ancient Egyptians are still used in divination today.

The methods of magic or divination described in this book have been adapted from the traditions of ancient Egypt. They are only suggestions, however, and each individual should try to find a practice that suits him- or herself.

Once you have decided to try some of the techniques described in this book, learn to focus your concentration on the symbols that you have chosen. Do not allow other thoughts to intrude,

Kom Ombu Temple.

and try to observe the symbols objectively. Closing your eyes so that you can reproduce the images in your mind is a good way to begin. Pay great attention to the impressions, thoughts and feelings that come to you and be prepared for an insight to remain hidden for some time after you have finished.

It is not advisable to tell fortunes or to use divination for others: it is a great responsibility, and your words may be misinterpreted. If you do give a reading, however, do not attempt to manipulate or influence anyone, even if your intentions are of the best.

Ancient Egyptian magic

As far back as the Fourth Dynasty, records show that magic was recognised and being practised by the ancient Egyptians. The ancient Egyptians firmly believed in the power of magic, which exerted a great influence over the everyday lives of the people, who invoked magic whenever issues of life, death, love, hate, disease and health arose. Because it was interwoven with both medicine and religion, it was routinely practised in the temples by priests.

Magical rites could apparently be performed at any time, although certain rules had to be observed. The magician always had to stand with his face pointing towards the east, for example; one spell had to be recited when the sun was setting at eventide; another required seven knots to be tied, starting in the morning and continuing at specified times until all seven knots were complete.

Timeline
Note that dates are approximate until 1570 BC.

Date	Dynasty	Events
3200 BC	First Dynasty	Menes unites Upper and Lower Egypt
2700 BC	Third Dynasty	Zoser: Imhotep builds the Step Pyramid at Saqqara
2600 BC	Fourth Dynasty	Cheops: the Great Pyramid at Giza; Khafra: the Second Pyramid and the Sphinx; Menkaura: the Third Pyramid
2080 BC	Eleventh Dynasty	The beginning of the Middle Kingdom
2000 BC	Twelfth Dynasty	The reign of Amen-em-het I The reign of Amen-em-het II
1570 BC	Eighteenth Dynasty	Ahmose expels the Hyksös and founds the New Kingdom
1490–1468 BC		Hatshepsut builds her mortuary temple at Der-el-Bahri
1468–1436 BC		Thutmose III builds temples and monuments.
1405–1367 BC		Karnak Thutmose IV uncovers the Sphinx; Amen-hotep III builds the temple at Luxor
1347–1339 BC		The reign of Tutankhamen
1309–1291 BC		The reign of Seti I

Date	Dynasty	Events
1308 BC	Nineteenth Dynasty	The reign of Rameses I
1290–1224 BC		The reign of Rameses II, 'the Great'
1224–1214 BC		The reign of Merneptah
1214–1190 BC		The reign of Seti II
1184 BC		The fall of Troy
1182–1151 BC	Twentieth Dynasty	The reign of Rameses III
570–526 BC	Twenty-sixth Dynasty	The reign of Amasis
c. 450 BC	Twenty-seventh Dynasty	The Greek historian Herodotus visits Egypt
332–30 BC	Thirty-first Dynasty	Alexander the Great and his successors rule Egypt
30 BC	(The Ptolemies)	The death of Cleopatra. Egypt becomes a Roman province

Magic and the deities of ancient Egypt

In ancient Egypt, magic began with the gods, who were considered to be the workers of wonders. Because, for the ancient Egyptians, there was no such thing as religion, their greatest deities were associated with magic, and perhaps our nearest equivalent to the belief of the ancient Egyptians is in magical power, which they believed came from the gods.

The Deities of Ancient Egypt

Deity	Association	Representation
Nun	Chaos and father of the gods	A person plunged up to the waist in water, arms held up
Atum	Spirit and ancestor of the human race	Man's head wearing the double crown of the pharaohs
Ra (or Re)	Creator and sun god	A royal child seated in a lotus or a man surmounted by a solar disc
Khepri	Scarab god of transformation	A scarab-faced man
Shu	The 'Atlas' of Egyptian mythology	The 'Atlas' of Egyptian mythology who holds up the sky
Tefnut	The twin of Shu and the goddess of dew and rain	A woman with the head of a lioness; dew and rain
Anhur	The sky-bearer	A warrior with a plumed headdress
Geb	The god of Earth and the physical foundation of the world	A woman wearing a rounded vase on her head; sky
Nut	The twin of Geb and goddess of the sky	A man swathed in mummy wrappings
Osiris	The god of the dead wrappings	A woman with a cow's head
Isis	The daughter of Geb and Nut, a protective deity	A man with the head of a fantastic mythical beast
Seth	The brother of Osiris and spirit of evil	Long, winged arms
Nephthys	The deity who watches over the bodies of the dead	A falcon
Horus	The divine falcon whose eyes are the sun and the moon	The daughter of Ra and a sky goddess
Hathor	The daughter of Ra and a sky goddess	A cow

The aim of the ancient Egyptians was to have the ability to command their deities to appear when they desired them to and then to work for them. Certain words or formulae used by trained men who practised magic, precious stones carried on the person or words inscribed on papyrus were believed to achieve the desired magical results.

Egypt was regarded as a nation of magicians from a very early period. Indeed, it is recorded in the Old Testament that Moses acquired his knowledge of magic from the Egyptians, being said to be 'learned in all the wisdom of the Egyptians and mighty in words and in deeds'.

The power to direct and control the movements of venomous reptiles (as illustrated by the story of Moses and the brazen serpent) was almost certainly known to the ancient Egyptians, and it has been reported that Egyptian magicians had perfected a method of compressing a viper's head to hypnotise it, whereupon it would become as stiff as a rod. Just like the Egyptian magicians, Moses and Aaron used rods to perform amazing feats. A Bible story tells how Moses stretched out his rod, whereupon there was 'hail and fire mingled with the hail, very grievous', while in another story, he commanded a plague of locusts.

An Egyptian priest-magician had to keep his practices secret and live a pure life; he would have been warned that he must not look at certain things. While the magician was a priest, the Egyptian physician could be a layman, and there are many papyri that contain incantations that are different from the remedy. Magical powers were ascribed to the drugs used in healing, which were believed to possess magical powers.

Images and figures were important in the practice of Egyptian magic, although the figures were not considered potent in themselves. First they had to be charged with magical power by means of an oral rite recited over them to ensure that they would be effective. Drawings on papyrus or other materials were sometimes used in the same way, while figures of the gods who were to be invoked were inscribed on the hand of an ailing patient before being licked off.

Magical charms – amulets – were usually attached to a person to ensure that they made contact with the body, which was believed to make them effective. The neck was generally chosen for amulets, and the string to which they were attached was usually tied with seven knots. Spells were also sometimes fastened to the left foot.

Amulets were carried as
powerful magical charms.

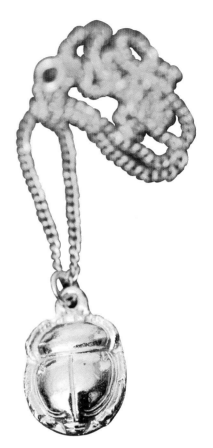

The magic of art

Egyptian art began to develop in
around 3000 BC, spanning two
thousand years overall, during which
time, some stylistic development
apart, there was remarkable
continuity, reflecting a deeply
religious and traditionalist society.

Both Egyptian sculpture and
painting are highly stylised, following
strict conventions and using symbols
of a religion that was centred on the
afterlife and the idealisation of the
dead, their servants, families and
possessions. Depictions of the human
form always show the face and
legs in profile, the upper torso
facing forwards, the hips three-
quarters turned, and the eye enlarged
and enhanced.

During Egypt's slow decline in power,
this style of art – both conservative and
subservient to religion – remained
unchanged. The level of technical
expertise continued to be high, and
artefacts were produced both
prolifically and almost constantly.

The practice of magic in ancient Egypt
was based on artefacts depicting the
gods, pharaohs, birds, animals, the sun
and the moon. Symbols were an essential
element in magical rituals and rites.

The art of ancient Egypt falls into three main periods: the Old, Middle and New kingdoms. Major collections of Egyptian art are found in Cairo, Egypt, and in London, England, where the art of the early dynastic period and the Old Kingdom is best exemplified by the monumental statue of the Great Sphinx at El Ga, dating from about 2530 BC. This gigantic figure of a lion with a human head, known as a sphinx, is carved from an outcrop of natural rock guarding the path to the pyramid of Khafra.

Isis shown in typical artistic style; in profile.

The depiction of gods and animals was an essential part of magical ritual.

A rich collection of grave goods survives from the period, including clothes, ornaments, jewellery and weapons, as well as many statues in stone and precious metals. The established stylistic conventions of painting show the human figure with head, legs, and feet in profile and the eyes and shoulders depicted frontally. Vivid wall paintings, such as Geese of Medum dating from about 2530 BC, show a variety of scenes from the everyday life of the time.

The Middle Kingdom, when Egypt was reunited under one ruler, is typified by tombs hewn from rock, attempts at realism in frescoes and deepened

Rameses II and Queen Nefertiti.

perception in portrait sculpture (one example is the head of Sesostris III). Typical of this period are sculptures of figures wrapped in mantles, with only their head, hands and feet showing.

The New Kingdom (1550 to 1070 BC) is represented by a much softer, more refined, style of painting and a fresh sophistication in jewellery and furnishings.

The golden age of the Eighteenth Dynasty (1570 to 1339 BC) saw the building of the temples of Karnak and Luxor and the maze of tombs in the Valley of the Kings. The pharaohs of the period, notably Akhenaton and Tutankhamen, inspired an extravagant style that was exemplified in the carved images of these god-like rulers: the statues of Akhenaton, the golden coffins of Tutankhamen's mummified body (which date from between about 1361 and 1352 BC) and the head of Akhenaton's queen, Nefertiti (dating from c. 1360 BC).

The monumental statues of Rameses II in Abu Simbel date from about the thirteenth century BC.

Ramses II Temple.

Religion and magic

What we today understand as Egyptian religion was a system of beliefs and practices. It originated in the worship of totemic animals, representing the ancestors of the clan, and was later superimposed with the abstract theology of a priestly caste.

The basis of Egptian religion

Suitable totems were traditionally kept as the symbols, or heads of, gods with complex attributes.

The hawk was sacred to the sun gods Ra and Horus.

The ibis was sacred to Thoth, the personification of wisdom.

The jackal was sacred to Anubis, the god of the lower regions and patron of embalming.

The cat was sacred to Bastet, who represented the sun's heat.

The god Bastet was represented by a cat.

The main cult was that of Osiris, god of the underworld. The story of Osiris, who was murdered, mourned by his sister and wife, Isis, and then rose again, was enacted in a fertility ritual similar to that of Tammuz, a Sumerian vegetation god.

Under the Eighteenth Dynasty, Amun, a local deity of Thebes, came to be regarded as the supreme god, in reflection of a rediscovered national unity. The pharaoh Akhenaton unsuccessfully attempted to establish the monotheistic cult of the solar disc as the one national deity. It remained the wish of all Egyptians to join Osiris in the Land of the West when they died.

According to Egyptian belief, immortality was conferred by the magical rite of mummification. Although this was originally the sole prerogative of the king, during the New Kingdom, mummification was extended to all who could afford it, people also being buried with the Book of the Dead.

The Book of the Dead, also known as the Book of Coming Forth by Day, dealt with funerary practices and was a guide to the soul after death through the Duat, the underworld. Survival in the afterlife was largely dependent on the preservation of the body, which required detailed methods of embalming and mummification. It was believed that the body and tomb contents were brought to life during a ceremony known as the Opening of the Mouth, and those who could afford it were buried with texts containing hymns and useful spells for their journey in the afterlife.

The Book of Gates described the divisions of the underworld and the gates through which the sun had to travel at night, each guarded by a being with a knife. The Book of What-is-in-the-Underworld depicted the twelve regions corresponding to the twelve hours of the night through which the sun travelled. Both texts can still be seen, inscribed on the walls of royal tombs dating from the New Kingdom.

Magical shabti statuettes were also buried with the dead and were believed to come to life in the afterlife and carry out any hard work for the deceased.

Amulets and symbols

Amulets were popular throughout Egypt's history and were believed to possess magical properties. Common designs included the scarab (which was often used as a seal, as well as an amulet), the symbol of the creator god Khepri; the ankh, the symbol of life; and the shen, a circle with a tangent, symbolising protection.

Amun and pharaoh.

Ancient Egyptian creation myths

Various Egyptian religious traditions and cults had versions of the creation of the world. At Heliopolis, it was taught that Atum first emerged on a mound from Nun, the watery primeval chaos, and then created Shu, air, and Tefnut, cloud, who joined together to create Nut, the sky, and Geb, the earth.

The Earth was thought of as being a flat disc floating on Nun, bounded by mountains supporting the sky.

Memphis tradition evolved a complex variant of this Heliopolitan theory, with the potter, Ptah, as the creator. As far as we know today, no detailed account of the creation of humans survives, but a few fragments that have been discovered suggest that Khnum, a ram-headed god, fashioned the first human on a potter's wheel.

The sun in ancient Egyptian religion

The sun was depicted in various forms. It frequently appeared as a red disc held between the forelegs of a scarab beetle. The disc represented the seed of new life contained in the sunrise, like the ball of dung in which the scarab wraps its eggs. Each morning the sun appeared between two mountains and travelled across the sky in a boat until it reached the west. Then it entered another boat and returned to the east, travelling beneath the earth.

Another version of the solar myth told that the sun was a child who had entered the mouth of the sky goddess and passed through her body to be born in the morning. The goddess was traditionally depicted as a heavenly cow, while the sun was represented as a calf. These variations were not mutually exclusive and could be combined, so that the sun god in human form is sometimes depicted sailing in his boat over the belly of the heavenly cow.

Hathor, the heavenly cow and wife of Horus, was an early deity who was later assimilated with the sky goddess.

Nephthys, the sister of Isis, may have also represented the sunset. After Osiris was killed by her husband Seth, the god of darkness, she mourned for Osiris in the form of a kite.

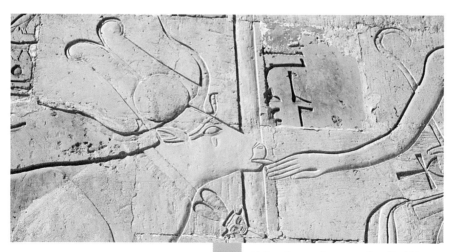

Hathor, the sacred cow, was the wife of Horus.

Horus was symbolised by a sacred hawk.

Anthropomorphism

During Egypt's prehistoric period, each area had its own deity, manifested in some animal or object. The gods who survived from this time into later Egyptian civilisation included Horus, Hathor, Anubis and Thoueris, a household deity and protector in childbirth, who was represented as a pregnant hippopotamus.

Thereafter there was an increasing tendency to identify the pharaoh with the falcon-headed god Horus, which led to the anthropomorphism (the attribution of human characteristics to animals, objectsor deities) that suffuses all Egyptian religion.

Gods were usually depicted with a human body, a name and the head of their associated animal. Ancient deities, such as Min, an early fertility god, and Ptah, however, continued to maintain the human form that they had had since prehistoric times.

The Greek historian Herodotus recorded in the fifth century BC that apes and other animals were kept in captivity by Egyptian priests. Although they were in no way regarded as idols, these animals were valued because they typified the various attributes of the Egyptian deities.

Montu, originally a local Theban god, on the left.

The development of ancient Egyptian religion

Unlike the Judaeo–Christian tradition, ancient Egypt did not have a fixed, organised system of religious beliefs. Neither was there a central, almighty deity. A series of gods and cults instead reflected the various strands of Egyptian belief and ritual that had developed at different times and places, much as in Roman and Greek religion.

Ancient Egypt was subdivided into nomes (administrative districts), each of which possessed its own triad of gods. As the country gradually coalesced politically, many of the local cults converged and gained widespread recognition. The triad of Osiris, Isis and Horus originally presided over a nome. Later, because of their popularity, they became national gods. Conservatism and compromise frequently led to the merging of old deities with those whose importance was rising, as illustrated by Ptah-Sokar and Amen-Ra.

The sun god Ra.

The winged disc symbolised Ra, Horus and the pharaoh.

Political developments had various impacts on the development of religion in Egypt. The mythological rivalry between the gods Horus and Seth, for example, probably reflected differing factions in early civil wars.

At Heliopolis, near Memphis, Ra was worshipped as the sun itself. By the time of the Fourth Dynasty, the pharaoh had become officially known as the 'son of Ra'. The winged disc, which was usually placed over temple doorways, represented Ra, Horus and the pharaoh.

During the Fifth Dynasty, the cult of Osiris was initiated in the Nile delta. According to traditional belief, Osiris was killed by his brother, Seth. In a struggle for power between the deities, Seth was eventually defeated by Horus, the son of Osiris, who then became king, Osiris rising to become ruler of the dead.

During the social revolution of the First Intermediate Period, the identification of a dead king with Osiris was extended to commoners. Indeed, 'Osiris' became a standard prefix to Egyptian names, indicating that the bearers were dead.

During the Eleventh Dynasty, Montu, originally a Theban god, assumed national importance based around the nobles of Thebes.

Isis, left.

Amun, the king of the gods (equivalent to the Greek Zeus and the Roman Jupiter), was originally an obscure god of Thebes who began to gain prominence only during the Twelfth Dynasty. After the victory of the Theban Eighteenth Dynasty, his cult expanded rapidly over the Hyksös, Amun merging with Ra to become Amen-Ra.

During the Late period, Amen-Ra was eclipsed and replaced as the ruler of the material world by Osiris. Isis gained ascendancy among the female goddesses, and the cult of their son, Horus the Child (Harpocrates), became popular.

During the New Kingdom, various foreign gods were venerated, including the Canaanite deities Reshef, a war god, and Anat, a goddess of love and war.

The arrival of the Greeks resulted in a further merging and blending of deities as similarities were perceived between Greek and Egyptian gods. Serapis, a fusion of Osiris and the Apis bull of Memphis, was created by the Ptolemies with the intention of promoting the unification of their Greek and Egyptian subjects, with Ptolemy I building the Serapeum, the temple of Serapis, at Alexandria. The cults of both Serapis and Isis spread to Greece, and later to Rome.

Some of the kings of Egypt, and a few of their subjects, were also deified. Imhotep, for example, who was the vizier of Zoser and the builder of the Step Pyramid, was worshipped during the Graeco–Roman period and was closely identified with Asclepius, the Greek god of healing.

Life after death and reincarnation

A deep mind has deep roots in nature – it will bloom many times over. But what a deep mind carries over into its next incarnation – perhaps in some remote sphere – is not its conventional merits and demerits, its load of remorse, or its sordid memories. These are washed away in its new baptism. What remains is only what was deep in that deep mind, so deep that new situations may again imply and admit it.

George Santayana 1863–1952
Spanish philosopher and critic. 'A Life of Reason' 1905–6

The ancient Egyptians believed in a world of the dead. They also believed that just as there were good and bad people on Earth, so there were good and bad souls in the underworld, while the funerary deities had both good and evil intentions. An essential condition for the continued life of the soul after death was the preservation of the body, which is why embalming was routinely practised from the very earliest days of the ancient Egyptian civilisation.

According to the solar religion, the pharaoh was either the physical son of Ra himself or an incarnation of Horus the Elder, the son of Ra. Although the Egyptians believed that, like the sun, the pharaoh would be resurrected after death, it remained important to pacify the gods of the underworld so that the dead king's soul, accompanied by food, servants and a collection of magic spells – the Book of the Dead – would

be assured of a safe passage through the twelve provinces of the underworld into eternal life.

As we have seen, the Egyptian religion did not have a creed that was laid down in a rigid formula. Through cult and usage, it was open to constant reinterpretation, which partly depended on external political or historical influences. It adapted itself to the needs of the individual worshipper and to the needs of the times. The search for new symbols was continuous, each one being considered to represent one facet of the truth. As these symbols changed over the centuries, shifts of emphasis in interpretation occurred.

How well it is that men should die, if only to erase their impressions and return clean washed.

Johann Wolfgang von Goethe 1749–1832
Source: Helion pub. 1999
From letters to Charlotte von Stein and
Christoph Wieland

The cult of Osiris

The position of Osiris as a god of the dead was fixed from a very early time. He was always represented as a dead king, that is, as a mummy bearing royal insignia.

A new pharaoh was not only regarded as the embodiment, or descendant, of Horus, but as Egypt's chief priest, who played a prominent role in the rituals surrounding the death of his father. The burial rites of the pharaohs were associated both with the daily rebirth of the sun and the resurrection of Osiris as a king in the afterlife.

When the burial rites spread to encompass the ordinary people of ancient Egypt, the cult of Osiris grew, at the expense of the practice of solar religion. Now all people, not only the king, hoped that they would enjoy eternal life. Osiris was the means by which they hoped to achieve this – his example represented hope, and he accordingly lost his original character, that of a frightening spirit of the underworld.

Tell me, what is Destiny preparing?
Tell me, why we two have
drawn so near? Aeons since, you
were my sister, sharing Kin with
me, or else my wife most dear.

Everything I am, my every feature,
You divined, my every nerve could
thrill, Read me at a glance – no
other creature Knows me as you
know, nor ever will.

Despite the change in their perception of Osiris, the ancient Egyptians clung to their traditions tenaciously, refusing to discard their beliefs completely. Most still felt that they should continue to pacify Osiris, who was also the judge of their souls, in order to satisfy him that a dead person was virtuous enough to be admitted to his underworld realm. In order to be assured of survival in the afterlife, people's complete identification with Osiris was indicated by copying the exact forms of his embalming. In addition, from the moment of death, a deceased person's name was prefaced with that of Osiris.

I cannot explain the significance to
me of this woman or her influence
over me, except by the theory of
metempsychosis. Yes, we were
once man and wife. Now our
knowledge of ourselves is veiled,
and lies in the spirit world. I can
find no name for us – the past, the
future, the All.

Seti 1 (ruled 1290–1279 BC). Defeated the Hittites in Syria and reconquered part of it. He was buried in a large tomb in Thebes. Seti's alabaster sarcophagus (similar to illustration) is in the Soane Museum in London.

The ancient Egyptian embalming process

Ritual embalming was a very complicated process that lasted about seventy days. Although some of the processes were degrading, they were thought to enable a dead person to take part in the passion of Osiris. All of the materials used in the embalming process were believed to have grown from the tears shed by the gods at the death of Osiris, their use conferring the power of these gods on the deceased.

When someone died, his or her body was removed from the house and taken to a special workshop or tent, which was called the place of purification. The body was carefully washed with water from the Nile and an incision was made in the left side so that the liver, lungs, stomach and intestines could be removed. The empty cavities were filled with balls of linen and the organs were placed in four Canopic jars. The brain was removed through the nostrils and the cavity filled with mud or linen packing to ensure that the features were preserved intact (if they disintegrated, it was believed that the personality would also disintegrate).

The heart, which was believed to be the seat of intelligence, was left in place. Then the entire body was soaked, first in salt and then in oils and resins. Amulets were arranged on the body, with a scarab being placed over the heart as a symbol of renewed life that would stimulate the deceased's eventual rebirth into eternal life. Finally, the body was wrapped in linen bandages and placed in a coffin.

I am certain that I have been here as I am now a thousand times before, and I hope to return a thousand times. . . it almost seems that our previous sojourns were too commonplace to deserve a second thought in the eyes of nature. . . I cannot deny that there may be higher natures than our own among the Monads. A World-Monad may produce out of the womb of its memories that which will prove prophetic, but it is actually a dim remembrance of something long expired. Similarly, human genius in a lightning flash of recollection discovers laws involved in producing the universe, because it was present when those laws were established. . .

When one reflects upon the eternity of the universe, one can conceive of no other destiny than that the Monads should eventually participate in the bliss of the Gods as joyfully co-operating forces. The work of creation will be entrusted to them. . . Man is the dialogue between nature and God. On other planets this dialogue will doubtless be of a higher and profounder character. What is lacking is Self-Knowledge. After that the rest will follow.

Johann Wolfgang von Goethe, conversation with Johannes Falk.

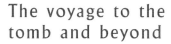

The voyage to the tomb and beyond

While the embalmers took on symbolic roles, the dead person's relatives had a special duty to attend every detail of the prescribed rites. This both proved how much they loved the deceased and kept an evil demon of the underworld at bay, preventing him from harming them and their children.

A great procession was formed as the mourners set off with the coffin, which was placed in a boat drawn by a sledge pulled by oxen and men, to go to the tomb. Following the chief mourners was a second sledge bearing the Canopic jars, with servants carrying all of the things that the deceased might need in the next world bringing up the rear. The ancient Egyptians firmly believed that magical powers in the form of wall paintings and papyrii would state the case of the deceased before his divine judge.

Tell me where dwell the thoughts
forgotten till thou call them forth?
Tell me where dwell the joys of
old? And where the ancient loves,
And when they will renew again,
and the night of oblivion past,
That I might traverse times and
spaces far remote, and bring
Comfort into a present sorrow
and a night of pain.

William Blake 1757–1827
Poet, artist, engraver and visionary
'Songs of Innocence' 1789

46

Dancers and musicians accompanied the procession to the tomb. During the course of the burial rites, a ceremony called 'Opening of the Mouth' was performed to open the way for the rebirth of the soul. Then the mummified body of the deceased was placed in a coffin. If his or her family had meticulously observed the precise rites of embalming, it was believed that the soul of the deceased would probably get as far as the hall of judgement in the underworld.

Man is not a product of the world of sense; and the end of his existence can never be attained in that world. His destination lies beyond time and space and all that pertains to sense.

Johann Gottlieb Fichte 1762–1814
German philosopher
'Critique of Religious Revelation' 1792

Once in the underworld, the soul of the dead person would be answerable for him- or herself to Osiris, who was generally regarded as representing the principle of good and as a just, kindly king, who had triumphed through his son over Seth, the embodiment of the principle of evil.

The least valid objection to the theory of soul circulation is that we forget these journeyings. Even during this life and without experiencing a 'change of clothes', multifarious conditions vanish from our memories. How then should we expect to remember the different bodies and the still more varied conditions experienced in previous lives? Why not allow a way of thinking to enjoy full light that a Plato, a Pythagoras, and the whole nations and eras have not disdained? . . . Let the soul return as often as it wishes. Certainly the earth is rich enough to bestow ever new gifts, new centuries, new countries, new minds, new discoveries and hopes.

Jean Paul Richter 1763-1825
German author
'Die Flegeljahre' (The Awkward Age) 1804–5

When the dead person had safely crossed the terrifying stretch of country between the world of the living and the kingdom of the dead, he or she was ushered into the presence of Osiris, 'The Good One', who was the judge of the dead. Entering into the hall of truths, he or she began the proceedings by reciting a negative confession. Then Thoth, the god of wisdom and reason, weighed the heart of the deceased against an ostrich feather. If the heart – the seat of truth – and the ostrich feather were of equal weight, the deceased had proved his or her innocence and would lead a life of eternal happiness in the kingdom of Osiris.

Our birth is but a sleep and a
  forgetting;
The Soul that rises with us, our
  life's Star,
Hath had elsewhere its setting,
And cometh from afar.
Not in entire forgetfulness
And not in utter nakedness,
But trailing clouds of glory do we
  come
From God who is our home.
Heaven lies about us in our infancy
Shades or the prison-house
  begin to close
Upon the growing Boy;
But He beholds the light, and
  whence it flows
He sees it in his joy.
The Youth, who daily farther from
  the east
Must travel, still is Nature's Priest,

And by the vision splendid
Is on his way attended;
At length the Man perceives
  it die away,
And fade into the light of
  common day.

Earth fills her lap with pleasures
  of her own . . .
The homely Nurse doth all she can
To make her Foster child,
  her Inmate Man,
Forget the glories he hath known,
And that imperial palace
  whence he came . . .
Though nothing can bring
  back the house
Of splendour in the grass, of
  glory in the flower . . .
Yet in my heart of hearts I feel
  your might . . .

William Wordsworth (1770–1850)
Ode. Intimations of Immortality (1807)

Egyptian magic essentials

Although the sacred rituals and traditions of Egyptian magic were passed down by word of mouth from priest to priest, their results were important enough to be recorded in ancient Egyptian texts. Many of these secrets have been carefully guarded to this day.

The eye of Horus was a symbol of light used to ward off evil.

Over the years, experts have unravelled many of these Egyptian practices and rites through archaeology and legend. You can discover some of the essentials of Egyptian magic for yourself and may decide that it is the perfect place from which to start on your own spiritual journey for the twenty-first century. Indeed, making magic based on the alleged mystery rites of the ancient Egyptians, the power of hieroglyphs and traditional amulets can enhance your life.

A large part of ancient Egyptian tradition reveals an intellectual side to old teachings, first expressed orally and then in written form using hieroglyphs. Amulets take us into the realm of the magic that the ancient Egyptians strongly believed in as a means of combating both the known and unknown forces of evil.

Some surviving magical texts written on papyrus have given us an idea of how widely people's lives were affected by superstitions and magic. We know that the divination of dreams was taken seriously, for example, because a long list of dreams and their meanings has been discovered in the Dream Book. Furthermore, each day had a magical significance attached to it, and calendars were made showing the significance of each day to help people to decide when it was safe to do certain things.

A wide variety of amulets was available to protect the individual against harm. Some took the form of deities, while others reproduced hieroglyphic signs symbolising abstract notions of magical power, such as beauty, prosperity, strength and life. A popular amulet was the eye of Horus,

the eye that had been knocked out by Seth, but that was later returned and healed by Thoth. A symbol of light, it was believed to ward off the evil eye.

Amulets such as 'magic wands' made of hippopotamus ivory and the cippi of Horus, which were not intended to protect against unknown evil forces, but against the very real presence of dangerous insects and animals.

Magic hippopotamus wands were designed to protect against poisonous scorpions and snakes approaching during the night. Their power came from the ivory of the hippopotamus, which was believed to be very potent because of the great strength of the

animal. The magic wands may have been used to draw magic circles around the bed before the occupant went to sleep, being laid under the bed during the night.

The cippi of Horus take the form of stelae (stone columns) depicting the child Horus holding harmful creatures, such as onyx gazelles (which were believed to have a baleful influence), lions, scorpions and snakes, while standing on two crocodiles.

Magic also affected the lives of the ancient Egyptians in the sphere of medicine, which was in many ways advanced for its time. Some medical papyrii survive that attempt to give

Thoueris, a household deity, was represented by a pregnant hippo.

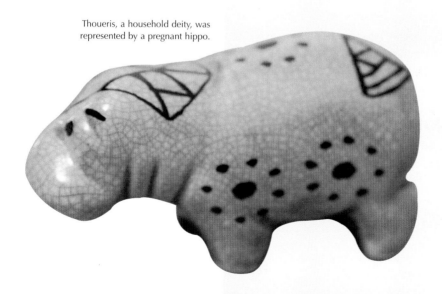

rational explanations when categorising different diseases, while almost modern procedures are described for examining, treating and predicting the outcome of patients' illnesses.

The Egyptians understood the importance of basic hygiene, rest and care, together with the uses of many natural drugs, and put their knowledge to the test in attempting to prevent the onset of certain medical problems. Although there were many gaps and errors in their knowledge of the human body, where their science failed them, magic took over. The power of suggestion probably had some effect, and the recitation of a spell could provide hope and comfort to the sick.

The magical protection of their gods and charms enabled the ancient Egyptians to enjoy their rich land, and all that it had to offer, for thousands of years.

A charm for exorcising headaches

O Re, O Atum, O Shu,
O Geb, O Nut, O Anubis,
In front of the divine shrine
O Horus, O Seth, O Isis,
O Nephthys, O Great Ennead,
O Little Ennead,
Come and see your father
concerning that enemy,
Dead man or dead woman,
adversary male or female
Which is in the head of
'N' born of 'M'.'
To be recited over a crocodile
of clay with grain in its mouth
And its eye of faience set
in its head.
One shall tie it up and
inscribe a drawing of the
gods upon a strip of fine linen
to be placed upon its head.

PART TWO

Divining with mirrors, colours and birds

Since the earliest days of primitive humankind, divination – foretelling the future – has been performed in various ways, both natural and artificial. This section of the book describes some of the magical systems of divination that were used in ancient Egypt, as well as providing practical examples.

The ancient Egyptians called upon deities for help when they performed their magical rituals, but the wisdom behind their rites came from natural earth energies and from the intuition that was deep within the practitioners themselves.

Exactly the same natural energies and powers can today help us to focus on a problem or goal in the same way as they did three thousand years ago in ancient Egypt. All ages and cultures have used the natural energies of magic

– fire, water, candles, herbs, trees, flowers, the sun, the moon and their cycles – to guide the lives of ordinary people. Ordinary household items, plants that can be found growing in almost any park or garden and a plain background can be used to perform simple divinations and rituals. No strange rites, no exotic locations and no magical artefacts are necessary.

In ancient Egypt, priest-magicians practised magic and interpreted the signs of divination on behalf of others (clairvoyants today perform the same function). But men and women have always carried out their own personal magical divination and rituals, especially at the times of the traditional festivals throughout the year. We all have the instincts and powers to perform magical rituals and divination, but in the modern world many people find it hard to trust their instincts and access their power.

Throughout the ages, the questions that people have asked have remained the same, namely those regarding issues of love, money and happiness. The techniques of Egyptian magic having survived, and being as accessible and relevant today as they ever were, if you trust yourself and your instincts, you will discover that the real power is within you and that you can use Egyptian magic to achieve your personal destiny, whatever that may be. Not only are these ancient forms of divination still powerful, they are remarkably simple to perform.

Hathor's magical mirror

Once, long ago in ancient Egypt, Hathor, the Egyptian goddess of love, music and dancing, was entrusted with the eye of the sun god, Ra, through which she could see everything. She always carried a shield that reflected things in their true light. This is what she used to make the very first magical mirror. One side of Hathor's mirror had the power of Ra to see everything, both near and far, in time and distance. The other side enabled people to see themselves in their true light – it was a brave individual who dared to look into this side of the mirror.

You do not need a magical mirror to practise the art of mirror-scrying. An ordinary, medium-sized hand mirror will do; you may prefer to use it exclusively for scrying and cover it with a soft cloth when you are not using it.

The best time to use mirror magic is during the hour before sunset. Place your mirror on a table in a quiet room where you will not be disturbed. Light two candles – which should be either pink or orange, the colours associated with Hathor – and place one on each side of the mirror. You will also need to burn some of Hathor's rose incense on either side of your mirror, which should be placed so that it faces a plain wall. Position the mirror slightly to one side so that you cannot see your own face reflected in it (unless you wish to see yourself in your true light).

Now clear your mind of everyday distractions. Sit quietly and allow pictures to form slowly, either in your mind's eye or within the mirror.

At the end of your session, cover your mirror carefully and remain sitting quietly alone while you allow the images to give you their own, special message.

Colour divination

Colour played an important part in ancient Egyptian magic, and for thousands of years the energies of different colours have been used in healing. In ancient times, the physical and psychological benefits of colours were well known, and today we can use these with great benefit. Did you know that blue helps to steady the respiration and lower blood pressure? Or that red raises the metabolic rate, orange aids digestion and stimulates the appetite, while pink can be used to create soothing environments in hospitals and prisons, thereby reducing anxiety and aggression?

It is well known that the effects of colour can affect us on a very deep, psychic level and that we can wear certain shades and tints of colour to access our inherent energies and powers. Crystals and talismans of appropriate colours can also be used to great effect in the use of colour magic.

Colours and their meanings

Colour	Meaning
White	The life force; divinity. For original ideas, clear vision and meeting the unknown.
Black	Regeneration; death. The colour of endings, carrying within them the seeds of the unknown.
Red	The essence of life; blood. For power, physical energy, determination and courage.
Orange	The fruits of the earth; the sun. For personal happiness, joy, health and fertility.
Yellow	Communication; the mind. Jealousy; treachery. For travel, learning and intellectual achievement.
Green	Love, emotion and the heart. For finding new love.
Blue	The spirit and healing. For limitless possibilities and conventional wisdom.
Purple	Sacred to Osiris. A link to inspiration, nobility of spirit and higher dimensions. For accessing the inner voice and spiritual strength.
Brown	The earth; elementals. For protection and affinity with the natural world.
Pink	Love and kindness. For harmony, reconciliation and inducing peaceful sleep.
Grey	Adaptability and compromise. For protection against psychic attack and invisibility. Use it to keep secrets and to avoid confrontation.
Gold	The sun; in ancient Egypt, the god Ra. For great ambitions, long life, money and the confidence to achieve one's dreams and to aim high.
Silver	The moon; in ancient Egypt, the goddess Isis. For fulfilment, visions and dreams outside the material world, magical insights and intuition

Using colour magic

Colour magic is best used to suggest strategies for success for subtle issues rather than for questions requiring 'yes' or 'no' answers. To use colour for magical divination, you can use coloured crystals, buttons or ribbons.

Place twelve different-coloured crystals, buttons or ribbons in a bag or box. Without looking inside, take out a single crystal, button or ribbon and note its colour. Replace it and then remove a second crystal, button or ribbon and note its colour. Now put that one back, remove a third and note its colour.

What the colours indicate

1 KEY ISSUE: The first colour tells you the real area of concern, which you may not be aware of.
2 OPPOSITION: The second colour indicates conflicting issues.
3 STRATEGY: The third colour suggests the best strategy for eventual happiness or success.

What the colours tell you

ISSUE	OPPOSITIONS	STRATEGY
White You, or someone close to you, feels restless and wants change in an important area of life.	Change threatens the status quo or feelings of insecurity.	Initiate change, but start slowly.
Black There is much unresolved business about.	Your doubts and fears are holding you back.	Take positive action to counteract negativity.
Grey Vacillation or being in a state of limbo.	Others' conflicting opinions are holding you back.	Adapt your plans to achieve some of your desires.
Red There is anger or resentment about a survival issue or another important matter.	Unnecessary confrontation could be about high anxiety levels.	Direct your anger into positive action.
Orange Core beliefs or an identity crisis.	Someone may be trying to dominate you.	Maintain your space. Do not attack others' egos.
Yellow Your mind or talents that are being spread too thinly.	Treachery or jealousy are undermining your efforts.	Prioritise. Be aware of what is being said about you.

ISSUE	OPPOSITIONS	STRATEGY
Green		
Make an emotional commitment. Follow your heart.	Subtle emotional blackmail may be around you.	Trust your own instincts. Do not listen to others.
Blue		
Are you considering an unconventional approach?	Someone close may be out to thwart you.	Stick to the rules. Use ingenuity to achieve your aims.
Purple		
There is a choice between deep emotional satisfaction and short-term gain.	Are unrealistic hopes holding you back?	Listen to your inner voices.
Brown		
The opinions of others or too much responsibility are draining your energy.	Those making demands or giving advice may be undermining your confidence.	Using your common sense will help you to off-load.
Pink		
Problems with keeping the peace are intruding on your personal life causing stress.	You are being forced to make choices that you don't want to make.	Withdraw from others' conflicts and concentrate on your personal space.
Gold		
You have a choice: aim for the stars or play safe and stay where you are.	Others say that you have reached your limits and refuse to see the possibilities open to you.	Set your own targets. Believe in yourself.

Magical birds

In ancient Egypt, the sun god, Ra, was the sign of resurrection that was symbolised by the fabulous, mythical phoenix, images of which were thought to ensure good health and a long life.

The main significance of birds in magical rites lies in the kind of bird, each type being associated with certain areas of life and specific qualities, such as health, money, love and other issues. A bird talisman in the form of a charm, ornament or etching can be used as a focus for magical divination, and the list below describes some of the birds that have traditionally been used in magical divination, which can still be of great value in the twenty-first century.

The magical meanings of various birds

Albatross
A bearer of burdens; a prophet of the weather. Killing one will bring a curse upon you.

Cockerel
Protection. A guardian when buried under the foundations of ancient buildings.

Crane
Good health and a long life. Rumoured to live for a thousand years.

Crow
Change or the need to move on. Traditionally a bringer of bad luck.

Cuckoo

A bringer of prosperity. On hearing the first cuckoo of spring, turn over the money in your pocket to ensure prosperity for the coming year. If heard on your right, you will soon be lucky with money, but if heard on your left, money will come more slowly.

Dove

Reconciliation; love. An ancient symbol of reconciliation and peace. A white dove flying around a house predicts a marriage or love match for someone in the family taking place soon.

Duck

Consolation. Hearing a duck quacking away from water indicates prosperity. Seeing ducks flying towards the sun promises happiness for those who are worried.

Eagle

Power and courage. Every ten years, according to ancient Egyptian lore, the eagle flew into the fires of hell. Soaring up with flaming feathers, the eagle plunged into the sea, thereby symbolising the renewal of life.

Falcon

Vigilance. A symbol of sudden disaster or the herald of sudden, unexpected change.

Goose

Domestic happiness. In ancient Egyptian lore, the goose laid the great cosmic egg containing Ra, the sun god, who brought light into the world.

Hawk

Enlightenment. Sacred to Horus, the god of learning, ancient Egyptian mythology told of the hawk as a bird of the sun that could soar towards its bright light without being blinded.

Hummingbird

Joy; truth. A bringer of happiness and harmony.

Ibis

Wisdom. This black-and-white bird was sacred to Thoth, the god of wisdom and learning in ancient Egyptian mythology, who was always depicted with the head of an ibis.

Kingfisher

Harmony. The bright-blue plumage of the halcyon bird, or kingfisher, is a promise of tranquillity for fourteen days after being sighted.

Magpie

A bringer of good news. As a divinatory bird, a single magpie is a bad omen, according to ancient tradition, but magpies have other significances, too:

'One for sorrow, Two for mirth,
Three for a letter, Four for a birth,
Five for silver, Six for gold,
Seven for a secret never to be told.'

Ostrich

Justice. Like the rhea and emu, which do not fly, the ostrich's significance in magical divination lies in the direction in which it runs. Ma'at, the ancient Egyptian goddess of wisdom and justice, wore an ostrich feather that was also used on the scales of justice as a counterbalance to the heart of a dead person.

Owl

Wisdom and learning. The owl is a traditional symbol of wisdom and learning and is also a bringer of bad tidings.

Peacock

Old people and lasting happiness. The peacock is an ancient symbol of immortality and also a weather prophet.

Pelican

Nurturing and motherhood. According to many ancient myths, the female pelican is famous for her maternal instincts.

Quail

Passion and fertility. The quail is a bird of fire that is also associated with the coming of spring, symbolises victory and valour and is said to possess great intelligence and powers of organisation.

Raven

Hidden potential and lost objects. Sometimes seen as a prophet of disaster, the raven is traditionally a guardian in times of danger and battle, as well as a protector of domestic property.

Robin

Compassion. Ancient myth says that the robin can grant wishes and that when a robin lives near a house or in a garden, those who live there are assured of good luck.

Seagull

Travel. Seagulls are said to be inhabited by the souls of dead sailors.

Stork

Babies and children. Storks are said to carry unborn babies from the salt marshes where they live to parents awaiting children.

Swallow

Consolation and revival. Sacred to Isis, the Egyptian mother goddess, the swallow is a symbol of awakening after the winter and of the renewal of life.

Swan

Creativity. Like the Egyptian goose, swans symbolise the cosmic egg and are believed to contain the souls of musicians, writers and poets.

Turkey

Altruism and self-sacrifice. Turkeys were traditionally known as creatures of sacrifice in ancient times.

Wagtail

Love. In traditional belief, the wagtail was associated with the creation of the Earth.

Wren

Ingenuity. In Christian tradition, it is considered lucky to see a wren on Christmas Eve.

Real birds have many mythical and magical connections and can be used as a focus for magic in bird divination. The most important source of information is found in the height at which they are flying, as well as the direction. In ancient times, bird divination, which was practised in most cultures, was an important means of interpreting messages from the sky. The direction and pattern of the birds' flight, their crowing, croaking or singing, indicated many different omens. The behaviour of both single birds and flocks can act as a focus for questions involving a course of action to be undertaken. Wait patiently for the birds to arrive before asking for a blessing and starting your interpretation.

The higher the birds are flying, the more favourable the answer to your question. A bird that flies directly upwards indicates that any venture should swiftly achieve success without you having to make much effort. If a bird veers up and down, landing and flying off again several times, or its flight is horizontal, you should not be put off by obstacles, but will need to put more effort into your venture.

If you see birds flying towards you from the right, confident action is indicated and a smooth passage for any coming venture can be expected. If they are flying from the left, delay is signified, and the birds may be suggesting that you remain silent or wait for a time. If birds are flying straight towards you, happier times are on the way, while birds flying away from you suggest that you should exercise caution and tact over the next few days, that you should delay

starting on a new venture and should spend time making plans instead.

A sudden change of direction indicates your own sudden doubts, inconstancy from someone close to you or a change of heart. If a bird hovers directly above you, this indicates that you must look out for new friends who are not being quite straight with you or that you should be aware that someone is criticising you behind your back.

The best time for hearing birdsong is at dawn, when you should close your eyes and ask a question. The dawn chorus will help you to form words and pictures in your mind, giving you your answer with their song. If you hear a bird sing as it takes flight, go ahead with a venture, while a bird calling as it lands is warning you to be more cautious. The scream of a bird of prey, or the call of a dark bird as it circles overhead, may be warning you of sudden opposition to your plans.

When there is more than one species of bird for your interpretation, one that is brightly coloured indicates that you should be prepared for immediate action, while a darker bird indicates delay. If your question involves several options, when a light-coloured bird arrives or moves, it indicates that you should take action; if it is a darker bird, however, you should delay or wait.

Another method of bird divination is to go outside into your garden, the nearest park or some other convenient, open space, to arrange twelve cards in a circle and to place some bird food on each card. Start by designating the first card either January or the current month and then ask when an event will occur. Now step back, stand still and watch to see which card a bird first pecks or lands on – this will tell you the name of the month (count the cards consecutively from the card that has been designated January or the first month). If the bird goes to a second card, this will tell you the month when the project or problem will end. Disregard any other cards that the bird may visit.

Finally, if you own a pet bird, remember that birds can access many levels of awareness, so that if your bird takes an instant dislike to a new friend or a stranger, it is giving you a warning that you should take seriously.

The magic of incense, fire and the moon

There are many other methods of magical divination apart from mirror-scrying, colour divination and bird divination, notably incense magic, fire magic and moon divination.

Incense magic

The ancient Egyptians used fragrances to awaken deep, magical impulses, and access to magical visions can still be achieved today by lighting incense sticks or cones, or by burning oils in a special burner. You may just enjoy sitting quietly alone as your chosen oil or incense releases its special fragrance into the atmosphere, or you may prefer to meditate. The spontaneous impressions that are imparted to you by fragrances can offer you an insight that goes far beyond those offered by the aural or visual senses.

An aromatic incense cone.

A variation of the magic practised by the ancient Egyptians is available today to evoke the energies of the different planets, that is, burning oils to release fragrances during your sun-sign month (the month of your zodiacal birth sign) or at any time when you need to remind yourself of your unique qualities and talents or to summon up your reserves of inner strength. A list of the fragrant oils associated with each zodiacal month appears on page 75.

Note that when you are using them for inhalation or massage, you will need to take great care when combining oils. If you wish to use two oils separately, it is quite safe to do so, however. The mixtures suggested here should be placed either in a standard oil-burner, which is warmed by a tea candle, or in a small dish placed over a warm radiator. To obtain the right fragrance for you, add the second oil to the first drop by drop until you have found the combination that you like.

Remember that lavender and rose oils will mix well with any other essential oil, while chamomile, geranium, frankincense, jasmine, rose, sandalwood, ylang-ylang and neroli all make fragrant combinations. Orange and lemon citrus oils are bad mixers, however, and should be used alone or according to specific instructions.

Sun-sign fragrances

Using the days of the week as a guide, you can also easily link a certain scent with the planets and thus tap into powerful, yet subtle, sources of energy for wisdom and healing.

Date	Zodiacal sign	Essential Oil
21 March to 20 April	Aries	Cedarwood or chamomile
21 April to 21 May	Taurus	Rose or patchouli
22 May to 21 June	Gemini	Lavender or lemongrass
22 June to 22 July	Cancer	Jasmine or eucalyptus
23 July to 23 August	Leo	Frankincense or cinnamon
24 August to 22 September	Virgo	Mimosa or rosemary
23 September to 23 October	Libra	Geranium or spearmint
24 October to 22 November	Scorpio	Myrrh or ginger
23 November to 21 December	Sagittarius	Sandalwood or orange
22 December to 20 January	Capricorn	Cypress or neroli
21 January to 18 February	Aquarius	Juniper or lemon
19 February to 20 March	Pisces	Pine or rosemary

The days of the week and planetary fragrances

Sunday: the day of the sun

Use frankincense, the fragrance of the sun, as an energiser.

Originating from the Middle East and Africa, frankincense was highly prized in all ancient civilisations. It mixes well with chamomile, another traditional oil of the sun.

The traditional oil and incense of the sun, frankincense can bring you visions of exotic places and sunny days, summer festivals, fire, vast, sandy deserts and nomads travelling with their camels and rich tents.

Monday: the day of the moon

Use jasmine, the fragrance of the moon, for dreams.

Mediterranean countries and India are the source of jasmine, which can be mixed with another moon fragrance, lemon. Jasmine oil is manufactured from many hundreds of flowers and is therefore very expensive to produce.

The flowers must always be picked during the night, when they give up their special fragrance, and only tiny quantities of oil can be made from them.

Visions of unicorns, fairy-tale castles and fairy folk may be seen when the scent of jasmine is released.

Tuesday: the day of action

Use pine, the fragrance of Mars, for invigoration and courage.

Pine oil was traditionally used to help with breathing problems. Wherever pine forests are abundant, pine oil is produced in equal abundance. It can be mixed with a few drops of Australian eucalyptus oil.

Burning pine incense or oil will bring visions of nature at its most magnificent and turbulent. Mountains and forests, winter celebrations and biting winds will be evoked by this fragrance, which imparts energy and courage.

Wednesday: the day of communication

Use lavender, the fragrance of Mercury, for soothing and uplifting.

Throughout the centuries, mind and body have always been soothed by the use of lavender fragrance. Originally only produced in Mediterranean regions, lavender is now almost universally grown. Mix lavender oil with the oil of geranium, another fragrance associated with communication.

Glimpses of exotic, distant places, far-off sounds of haunting music, soft silks, brilliantly coloured domes tipped with gold and fragrant spices may be evoked when you choose to burn lavender and geranium oils on a Wednesday.

Thursday: the day of ancient rituals

Use sandalwood, the fragrance of Jupiter, for wisdom and healing.

Sandalwood, which comes from India, is used for carvings. The oil of sandalwood was a traditional ancient Egyptian incense and can be mixed with neroli, another oil associated with healing and ancient rituals.

To see scenes of processions, shrines, slow rituals, pageants and ornamental temples, and to evoke deep spiritual healing, burn the incense of sandalwood.

Friday: the day of love

Use rose, the fragrance of Venus, for peace.

All cultures have traditionally associated the rose with love. Rose oil, which is today made from flowers grown in France, China and Morocco, can be mixed with another oil of love, ylang-ylang.

For visions of romance and scenes of passion, images of family members, present and future lovers, burn rose oil, the fragrance of love.

Saturday: the day of immortality

Use cypress, the fragrance of Saturn, for preservation.

The oil of the cypress was traditionally associated with symbols of immortality by the ancient Egyptians, who used it to preserve the body in its tomb. Cypress oil can be mixed with patchouli, another Far Eastern fragrance.

To access visions of houses and schools full of industrious people, images of home life and work, domestic cleaning and cooking, burn cypress oil, the fragrance of industry and accomplishment.

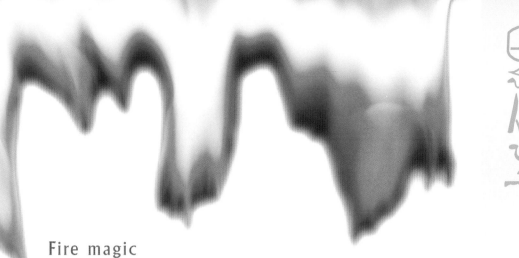

Fire magic

The discovery of fire transformed life in every ancient culture: fire enabled people to cook their food, kept them warm, shaped metals and, very importantly, protected them from wild animals. There are many myths concerning fire, and fire festivals are central to cultures throughout the world. The transformation of sacrifices – symbolic or animal – through fire into ashes, those ashes then being returned to the soil, was thought to endow the soil with continuing life.

The art of divination by fire is known as pyromancy. Unpredictable and changeable, fire was regarded as the perfect medium for interpreting omens in ancient times. The most potent fires to study were thought to be those intended for sacrifice, and a vigorously burning fire that consumed fuel

quickly was considered to portend a promising future. If a sacrificial fire was clear, with transparent flames that crackled, it was supposed to be a good omen. A silent, slowly burning fire that did not consume the sacrifice efficiently indicated that coming events and days would be unpropitious, however.

Although few of us today believe that disaster or great fortune can be foretold by watching a fire, studying flames and reading the pictures created by sparks and embers is a very evocative way of visually awakening our inner knowledge and wisdom. Many of us can recall that as children we saw magical kingdoms and fairies in the flames, and this ability – known as scrying – often lies dormant when we reach adulthood.

Try lighting a small fire in your grate or a bonfire in your garden. Then sit quietly, letting your intuition guide you as you watch the flames and ask questions about the general direction of your life or more specific questions. However the answers come, be it in the form of general impressions, pictures or words, never doubt your fire wisdom – it comes to you from one of the most ancient of magical traditions.

Interpreting the flames

Flames can send you many messages.

If you light a fire and it catches immediately and flares upwards, a venture that you may be planning will swiftly take effect.

If a fire burns slowly, it indicates that you may need to persevere to get a venture off the ground.

■ A fire that refuses to light denotes that you should seek another approach to your chosen venture.

■ Clear, red flames that crackle promise success and happiness. If you are confident and listen to your inner voice, guidance will come.

■ Dull, silent, yellowish flames are telling you that you have opposition and obstacles to overcome.

■ A fire that spits warns you of someone who is unexpectedly envious of your activities.

■ Quickly consumed fuel tells you that it will not be long before you see the results of your venture.

■ A slow-burning fire indicates delays.

■ Flames that appear to be blown by the wind and to burn in one direction tell you that confusion abounds or that you may be under pressure to conform.

■ A fire that goes out suddenly indicates that you may be left to do things on your own. If your venture is important, this should not put you off, however.

Understanding the smoke

Watching a smoking fire can tell you a number of things.

■ When the smoke rises directly upwards, you should be aiming high.

■ Smoke blowing in one direction tells you that you may be faced with a choice – between two people or courses of action – and that one is more favoured than the other.

■ If the smoke is thick and choking, avoid making a decision when you are uncertain of your facts, and do not be diverted from the main issue. Be warned that others' opinions may be unreliable.

■ When the smoke is evenly spread, it is telling you to balance conflicting demands and not to make a choice between one or the other.

Seeing pictures

As you sit looking into the constantly flickering flames, you may see moving pictures. Perhaps you can see people, boats or houses. Sometimes the images change rapidly, but try to recognise what each different image suggests. You may be seeing a coherent message or picture, but if you aren't, write or sketch notes of the images. Before you go to sleep, look at your notes, and when you wake up, read them again. However unlikely it may be, these images hold a message for you.

Glowing embers produce equally vivid images: pieces of wood or coals may connect, apparently forming islands, bridges or towns, for example. Use these images to discover the story of your real world and to find out how it may be enriched.

Reading the ashes

Images in the ashes offer further scope for divination.

■ Take a scoop and shake the cold ashes onto a piece of white or black paper. The image formed will come from deep within you. Don't worry about ascribing the image a conventional meaning. If you see a boat, bird or butterfly, for example, your subconscious will suggest a meaning.

■ What is the shape of your fire? If it is a circle, this indicates harmony. A square shape tells you that you must fit your dreams into the present and should not wait for tomorrow. An irregular shape, perhaps a triangle, tells you that new possibilities may lie ahead. A heap of ashes is telling you that you should build a mountain to climb. Ashes that take the form of specific birds or animals have their own symbolic meanings, with each different shape sending you a unique message.

■ You can bury any sorrows or regrets that are holding you back by collecting the cold ashes of your fire and burying them in the ground. Plant a seed – an acorn will do nicely – on that spot and allow the new wood to grow over, and rise above, your past.

The rabbit is traditionally regarded as a symbol of good fortune and this ash outline represents success in making money.

Moon divination

All cultures throughout the world have traditionally regarded the moon as mysterious, intuitive and feminine (and the moon's close relationship with nature, the female cycle and rhythms of life are well known to us), which is why the lunar deities of many ancient cultures tended to be goddesses.

The first moon goddesses were depicted in Europe in Stone Age or Neolithic cave paintings – lasting from about 7000 BC to around 5500 BC. In these images, the moon was seen to have three main phases: waxing, full and waning, echoing the stages of human existence – birth, maturity and death.

Isis (left) holding a
papyrus sceptre.

The lunar cycle was especially identified with women, when its three phases represented the maiden, the mother and the wise woman or crone. If a woman wanted to become pregnant, she would sleep under the rays of the moon as it waxed and became full, believing that this ensured conception.

When the hunter-gatherer way of life was gradually overtaken by the advent of agriculture, the fertility of the moon goddess became identified with the earth's fecundity. The night was regarded as being ruled by the moon goddess, who was worshipped in tandem with the sun god, the ruler of the day, as the joint sources of all goodness and life.

In ancient Egypt, Isis was both the mother of the sun and a moon goddess.

The symbols of life that she was depicted holding were a papyrus sceptre and the ankh, the traditional symbol of life.

The Egyptians also venerated a moon god, Khonsu ('He who Crosses the Sky'), who was pictured as a mummified youth, crowned with both a full moon and a crescent moon, holding a crook, sceptre and flail. Khonsu was associated with pregnancy.

Because it disappears from the sky for three days at the end of each cycle and reappears as a visible crescent, the moon became associated with rebirth. Popular myths told that the moon took the souls of the dead back to her womb to await fertilisation by the sun before being reborn.

Moon magic

When you decide to begin your own moon magic, choose a night when the moon is visible in the sky. At the start of the lunar cycle, the crescent of the waxing moon can be seen on the right of the moon, and each night the visible part of the moon grows larger from right to left, until it is completely illuminated. When the full moon begins to wane, darkness increases from the right, gradually covering the light on the left, until the moon disappears completely. Three days later, the moon reappears as a crescent.

Isis was a goddess of the moon.

■ The phase of the waxing moon has long been considered a time of increased money, new love, happiness, growth and healing rituals.

■ A full moon is traditionally associated with success in money, fertility and love, and this lunar phase is said to be a good time to begin a new job or get married.

■ The waning moon is associated with the power to cure illness and bad habits and to reverse unhappiness, also offering the opportunity to break unwanted ties or associations.

■ The period of the dark moon, when the old moon is invisible to us, is believed to be a good time to carry out any secret undertakings and protection rituals.

Measured from one new moon to the next, the lunar cycle lasts for 29.5 days, it taking a little more than 27 days for the moon to complete its orbit around the Earth. If you want to calculate the phases of the moon, you can count one lunar month as lasting 28 days. On a calendar, the lunar month is divided into four weeks, beginning with the week of the new moon, then the week of the first quarter, followed by the week of the full moon and then the week of the last quarter. Each quarter period will vary between seven and eight days, according to the month, the lunar month also varying slightly each year. There are eight recognised phases within the lunar cycle, and to identify the phases of the moon more accurately before beginning your moon magic, consult a diary or daily newspaper.

How moon magic works

Since prehistoric times, moon magic has worked using three aspects of the moon: the waxing moon, the full moon and the waning moon. Each fluid phase lasts for about nine nights, beginning when the first crescent moon appears, which is the most magical of times.

When determining moon phases, be governed by your intuition, not your calendar. The rhythmical influence of the moon can be felt within you, so always go with what you feel and not with what the calendar dictates. Sometimes, for example, the surge that you feel at the time of the full moon will last a few days longer than the calendar indicates, in which case, go with it and take advantage of your extra energy boost to complete your tasks.

You will eventually find that your personal cycle echoes the energies of the moon as they ebb and flow. An increase in your enthusiasm and energy will be linked with the new moon, reaching a peak on the crescent and increasing to their greatest momentum at the time of the full moon. Thereafter, your energy will begin to recede and you may begin to tire easily and feel unaccountably irritable as the waning period starts. This is the time to avoid any unnecessary conflict and to make sure that you get more rest. When the waning moon dies, ensure that you withdraw both mentally and physically into a time of reflection. In the near future, the next crescent moon will offer you another chance to achieve whatever it is that you desire.

Magic for the new and waxing moons

New moon, true moon

Silver you grow,

Let now my fortune

Increase show.

Choose the time of the new and waxing moons to initiate any new venture.

On the first day of a new moon, use money rituals to increase your wealth by first selecting a silver coin (symbolising the colour and metal of the moon). Standing at an open window, face the crescent moon, but do not look directly at it. Recite the verse above, then light a silver candle and hold the silver coin in your right hand to bring action into your life. Turn over your silver coin and visualise silver coins showering down upon you like moonbeams. Blow out your candle and picture the silver light spreading abundance and prosperity over any venture in which you are involved.

Until the moon becomes full, create and add to a pile of silver coins each day in this way. At the time of the full moon, buy someone close to you a small gift or give your collection of coins to a charity or another good cause. Do this, and you will discover that your gift will be returned to you many times over.

Magic for the waning moon

Old Moon,

Wane Moon,

Moon of Sorrow,

Bring me now

A new tomorrow.

If you have been experiencing a time when your health has not been good or you have had a run of bad luck, this can be a very potent lunar phase during which to reverse your problems.

When the moon is starting to wane, go to a pond or lake on a clear night and look for a white stone. Using a silver-handled knife or black stone, scratch a symbol such as a spiral, cross or square on the stone to represent your negative feelings, ill health or sadness. Now recite the above verse as you throw the stone into the water so that it causes the reflection of the waning moon to ripple.

According to magical tradition, you must always replace what you remove, so to replace the stone, plant some seeds next to the pond or lake to represent a new beginning.

Magic for the full moon

Lady Moon,
Bring to me
My lover,
Whether of high degree,
Low estate
Or gypsy wild,
Close to home
Or cross the sea.
Let me dream
My lover's face,
My future home,
Our first-born child,
And show me
Where my love will be.

The time of the full moon is a particularly potent time for matters of the heart or love magic.

When the moon is full, cut a small willow twig using a silver-handled knife, then take it home and hang it from a silver ring. Light some sandalwood or jasmine incense. Now pass the ring through the fragrant smoke sending out strong and loving feelings as you place the ring on your wedding finger. Visualise the face of either the person whom you would like to meet or your absent lover as you put the ring underneath your pillow and recite the verse above.

Relax and go to bed. Make sure that you sleep with the moonlight shining on your pillow to ensure that you dream of your future love. The next day, take the willow twig and plant it near water.

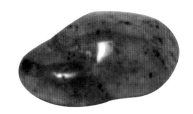

Items associated with the moon

Any of the items listed below, all of which are associated with the moon, can be used when making lunar wishes or performing lunar rituals. You could also hold a silver coin or burn a silver candle to focus your energies for visualisation purposes.

Association with the moon	Item
Colour and metal	Silver
Element	Water
Astrological sign	Cancer
Sea creature	Crab
Precious stones	Sea-green aquamarine, pearl, beryl and moonstone (of various colours)
Flowers	Jasmine, gardenia, dog rose, night scented stock and wallflower
Herbs	Lemon balm, poppy seed and myrrh
Animals	Dog and wolf
Bird	Owl
Trees, plants and fruits	Mountain ash, willow, rowan, cactus, mango and banana
Angel	Archangel Gabriel

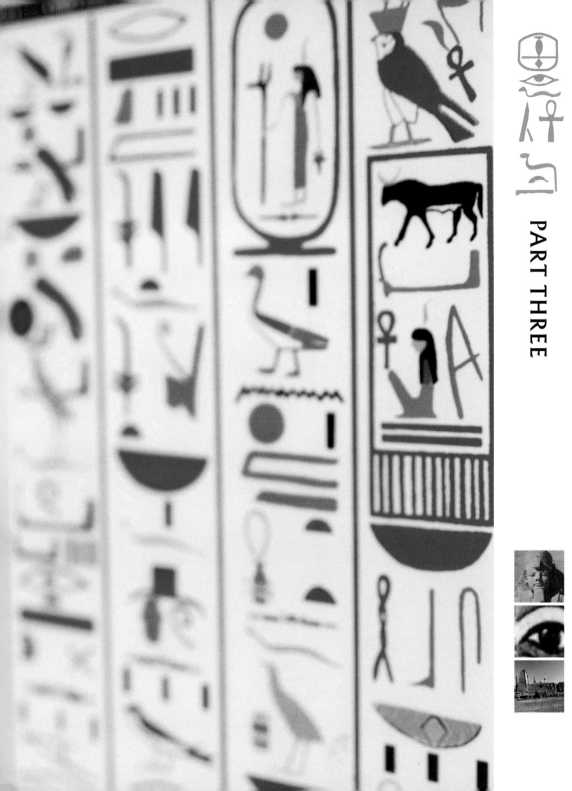

PART THREE

Stories of Egyptian magic

Ancient Egyptian legends suggest that books on magic once existed that were written during a period of antiquity. These, however, are now unknown.

Approximate date	Dynasty	Story
2600 BC	Fourth Dynasty	'The Golden Lotus'
		'Teta, the Magician'
1290–1224 BC	Nineteenth Dynasty	'The Book of Thoth'
		'Se-Osiris and the Sealed Letter'

'The story of the golden lotus'

Pharaoh Khufu's father, Seneferu, had reigned over Egypt for many years. His subjects were contented and life was peaceful. There was little state business because there were no foreign wars to fight, and Seneferu often found that time was hanging heavily on his hands. His great achievement had been to build the Great Pyramid at Giza.

One day Seneferu was wandering through his palace at Memphis, feeling bored and out of sorts. Suddenly he thought of Zazamankh, his chief magician. 'He is the only man who can find something to entertain me with. He is a wise scribe of the scrolls and will be able to show me something I have never seen before.' Seneferu clapped his hands. 'Send Zazamankh to me!' he commanded.

Seneferu's servants hurried to the House of Wisdom, where they found Zazamankh and told him that the pharaoh commanded his presence immediately. When the servants had brought Zazamankh to the pharaoh, Seneferu said to him, 'I have been looking for something to interest me all over the palace, but I can find nothing. What can you think of that will interest me?'

'Life, health and strength to you, pharaoh! I suggest that you embark on a voyage that will be different from anything you have ever experienced before. Prepare to sail down the Nile to the lake below Memphis – but you must remember to do exactly as I advise you.'

'I am sure that you are going to show me some marvellous things,' replied Seneferu, 'but I am tired of sailing on the lake and down the Nile. However, I will do as you suggest and order the royal boat to be made ready.'

93

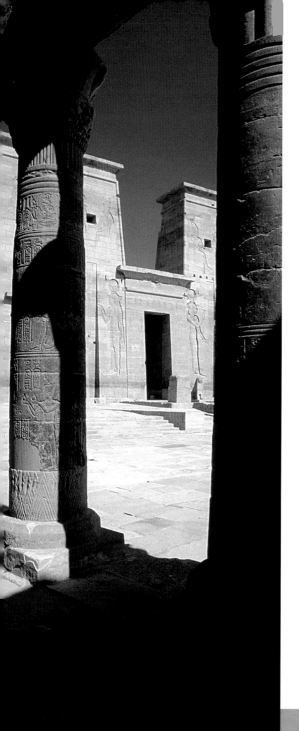

'I assure you,' Zazamankh replied, 'that this will be no ordinary voyage. To begin with, your rowers will be quite different from any you have ever seen before because they will be beautiful maidens chosen from the Royal House of the King's Women. And while you are watching the birds on the lake and see the green grass growing on the banks and the flower-filled fields as you are being rowed down the river, you will feel at ease as never before.'

'Well, this will be a new experience' said the pharaoh, who was beginning to feel intrigued by the prospect. 'I will put you in complete charge of this journey. Make all of the necessary arrangements immediately.'

'Bring me twenty oars,' Zazamankh ordered the pharaoh's attendants, 'which must be made of ebony inlaid with gold and have blades made of light wood inlaid with electrum. To row the royal boat, choose twenty of the most beautiful girls in the pharaoh's household. Ensure that they are young, slender and have long, flowing hair.' 'Each of these young girls must have a net made of golden thread to wear as a dress, with gold ornaments decorated with electrum and malachite', Zazamankh added, and the attendants hurried to begin their tasks.

Once everything was prepared, the pharaoh embarked on the royal boat and the beautiful girls began to row him down the river and out on to the lake. Seneferu was delighted by the sight and sound of so many delightful girls, and began to wonder if he was actually in paradise.

Suddenly one of the girls, who was steering in the raised stern of the royal boat, was accidentally knocked on the head with an oar by her partner and the golden lotus that decorated the fillet binding her hair was swept into the water and immediately sank. The singing stopped as the girl gave a cry and leant over the side of the boat to look for her golden lotus. As she stopped rowing, so did all of the other girls behind her.

'Why have you stopped rowing?' called the pharaoh in alarm. 'Our steerer has stopped rowing and we have no one to follow', replied the girls.

'Why have you stopped steering and singing?' Seneferu asked the girl. 'Please forgive me', she sobbed. 'An oar accidentally hit my head and my golden lotus was swept from my hair into the water. I shall never find it again.'

'Continue rowing and singing', commanded the pharaoh. 'I will give you another golden lotus.' 'No,' wept the girl, 'I want no other golden lotus but my own.'

'There is only one person who can find your golden lotus, which has surely sunk to the bottom of the lake. He is my magician, Zazamankh', said the pharaoh. 'It was he who thought of this voyage.' 'Bring him to me immediately!' he commanded his attendants.

The pharaoh's attendants brought Zazamankh to the royal boat. As the magician knelt before Seneferu, who was sitting in his silken pavilion, the pharaoh said to him, 'My brother and friend, I have done as you advised me. My eyes are delighted by the spectacle of these beautiful rowers, and my royal heart has been refreshed. I feel as though I am sailing back into the golden days of old, when Ra ruled the Earth, as we sail up and down the lake. The singing, the flowers and the trees remind me that the good god Osiris will one day return from Duat. But one of these beautiful girls has stopped singing to me because a golden lotus has fallen from her hair to the bottom of the lake. The other girls cannot row in time any more and she won't be comforted with my promises of any other gift. All she does is weep for her lost golden lotus.'

Zazamankh listened carefully and then replied, 'My lord, may you have health, strength and life always! I will

95

do as you ask and return the golden lotus to your beautiful girl. For to a magician such as I, this is no great feat to perform. Perhaps it will be an enchantment that will amaze you.'

Standing at the stern of the royal boat, Zazamankh chanted words of great power and magic spells. He held out his wand and suddenly the waters of the lake, which were at least twenty feet deep, parted, as if a great sword had cut through them. In front of the pharaoh's eyes a huge cliff of water, at least forty feet high, rose up and the royal boat slid down into the gap that it had left. Drifting on the bottom of the lake, they came to a huge, open space, which was as dry and firm as the land. There, in front of the boat, lay the golden lotus. The girl saw it and gave a cry of joy. She jumped over the side of the boat, picked up the lotus and tucked it back into her hair before quickly climbing back into the boat, taking her place and picking up her oar.

As Zazamankh lowered his wand, the royal boat slid slowly up the side of the cliff of water and soon they were level with the surface of the lake. Another magic word returned the cliff of water to its original place. The evening breeze rippled gently on the still surface of the lake as though nothing had happened.

'You are the greatest of all magicians, Zazamankh', cried the pharaoh, who was amazed. 'Today you have shown me the most astonishing wonders, and I will reward you with anything that you desire.'

The royal boat slowly continued on its way across the lake. Everything glowed in the evening light of the setting sun. As they dipped their ebony and silver-coloured oars into the water, the beautiful girls, dressed in their shining clothes of golden net, with their glossy black hair adorned with bejewelled golden lotus flowers, sang an ancient love song of old Egypt in their clear, sweet voices:

She stands upon the further side,
Between us flows the Nile,
And in those waters deep and wide
There lurks a crocodile.
Yet is my love so sweet and true,
A word of power – a charm,
The stream is land beneath my feet,
And bears me without harm.
For I shall come to where she stands,
No more be held apart.
And I shall take my darling's hands,
And draw her to my heart.

As the light faded, the sound of the girls' singing echoed across the lake, and Pharaoh Seneferu rewarded Zazamankh with a place at his right hand for the rest of his life.

'Teta, the magician'

The building of the Great Pyramid at Giza in Egypt was begun during the reign of Pharaoh Khufu [also known as Cheops], who was believed to be an incarnation of the spirit of Amen-Ra. Hemon, the architect, had absorbed all of the knowledge available about Imhotep, who had built the Step Pyramid a hundred years before for Pharaoh Zoser. During the inundation months each year, thousands of farmers came and laboured in the building of the Great Pyramid.

Neither Hemon nor all of the magicians of Memphis could find the original papyrus that Imhotep had left containing the magic words that would keep a pyramid safe, however, and people were frightened that Seth, the evil one, would use his weapons of thunderbolts and earthquakes to destroy the magnificent pyramid.

Messengers offering rewards were sent out across Egypt to search for the secret words of power. From Thebes through Heliopolis to Abydos, magicians were urged to look carefully through all of their spells and incantations. In all of the temples, from Tanis to Phiae, priests searched their ancient records. Nothing was found.

The pharaoh was distraught until one of his sons, Hordedef, approached him one day. 'Life, health and strength to you my father, pharaoh of Egypt! I have wonderful news for you. Not far from here, at Meidum, which is close to the pyramid of my grandfather, Seneferu, I have discovered a magician who is one hundred and ten years old. He is the most amazing magician in your entire realm and his name is Teta. As a boy he lived during the reign of Zoser and knew about the building of the pyramid that Imhotep built. Every single day he eats a whole side of beef and five hundred cakes of bread and drinks one hundred draughts of beer.' 'I am delighted to hear this news, my son', replied Khufu. 'Tell me more.'

'He can make the most savage desert lion follow him as tamely as a dog. He knows the magic to restore a head that has been cut off and, what is more, he swears that he knows how to find the papyrus that you are searching for. It is indeed inscribed with the charms that must be said and the words of power that will keep a pyramid safe from Seth, the evil one', said Prince Hordedef.

'So we can protect the pyramid from destruction if we have this papyrus?' asked the pharaoh. 'Yes, indeed, my lord', replied his son. 'Then go immediately. Make sure that you take my royal litter and as many servants as you need. Bring back this magician called Teta. Treat him as though he were visiting royalty and make sure that he has every comfort during your journey up the river Nile.'

Hordedef set off straight away. When he arrived at the pyramid of Meidum, he landed and proceeded up the royal causeway until he reached the pyramid. Beyond it, in a small village, he found the house where Teta, the magician, lived. The old man was lying on a palm-wood couch in the shade of his house. His servants were anointing his head and feet with sweet-smelling oil and fanning him with palm leaves.

Reverently saluting him, Prince Hordedef addressed the magician. 'Teta, the magician, I bring you greetings and a message from my father, the great pharaoh Khufu, to whom be life, health and strength! We salute your revered great age and pray that you may continue to be free of all of the infirmities of age. My father invites you to pay him a visit and has sent his own royal barge for you to travel in comfort and ease. He desires that you join him at Memphis to share his excellent food and wines. I have brought his royal litter, which is made of ebony set with gold, to carry you like a pharaoh from your home to the royal barge so that

you may travel to the palace in Memphis where my father awaits you.'

'Peace be with you,' replied the magician, 'and life, health and strength to your father Khufu, the pharaoh! May he give you the highest place among his councillors, may you be protected against your enemies and may you be shown the road of righteousness that leads through the desert to Duat and to the throne of Osiris. Yes, I will gladly come with you. Please arrange for a second boat to bring my precious books and my attendants.'

The magician and his entourage accordingly set sail down the river Nile with Prince Hordedef and in due course arrived at the palace in Memphis. 'Bring the magician to me immediately', commanded Khufu when he heard of his son's return.

Sitting on his splendid throne, Khufu welcomed Teta, the magician, in the great hall of columns, surrounded by all of the great men of Egypt, who were eager to see him. 'How is it, Teta, great magician, that I have never seen or heard of you before?' enquired the pharaoh. 'Life, health and strength to the good god Khufu, Pharaoh of Egypt, who has sent for me!' replied Teta. 'Behold, I am here. He who is summoned is he who comes', he said as he bowed low.

'Is it true that the rumours that I have heard about all of your magical powers can be verified?' asked the pharaoh. 'Indeed, they can,' replied the magician, continuing, 'remember that I am a hundred and ten years old and full of wisdom.'

'Bring a prisoner who has been condemned to execution,' commanded the pharaoh, 'and let the executioner come, too.' 'Oh pharaoh!' cried the magician. 'Not a man, I beg you. Order the head of some other living creature to be cut off.'

'It shall be so', agreed Khufu. 'Bring a duck and cut off its head.' The duck's head was accordingly cut off and laid at the opposite end of the hall to its body. As Teta cast a secret charm and spoke powerful magic words, the duck's body fluttered across the hall towards its head, which moved towards it until they were rejoined. Flapping its wings furiously, the duck began to quack loudly.

Teta's magic was repeated on a goose and an ox, with exactly the same results. 'It is true, Teta,' marvelled Khufu, 'you are indeed the greatest of all magicians. Now,' he continued, 'can you tell me what I am anxious to discover? Where is the papyrus containing the words that Imhotep wrote that have the power to protect the pyramids that he built for my father, the pharaoh Seneferu, and also for Zoser?'

'Yes, I can indeed', replied Teta, continuing, 'hidden in the great temple of Amen-Ra at Heliopolis is a flint casket. It contains the papyrus that you seek. I cannot reveal where the casket is hidden, but my magic can tell you the identity of the one person who will be able to find it for you.'

'Your reward will be beyond your wildest dreams', cried the pharaoh in excitement. 'Tell me his name!' 'Tonight,' replied Teta, 'a priest's wife called Rud-didet will give birth to three children at Heliopolis who will bear the spirit of Amen-Ra. One of these three children will sit where you are sitting and will rule over Egypt, and one of them will find the casket.'

The pharaoh was very disturbed. 'Only by an act of treason can one of them become a pharaoh of Egypt', he said. 'Perhaps it would be wiser quickly to send someone to Heliopolis to kill Rud-didet before her children are born.'

'No', said Teta firmly, 'your son will rule after you, and his son, Menkaura, after him. It will be many years before a son of Rud-didet sits on the throne of the Upper and Lower Lands of Egypt. Only this child can find the casket containing the words of power, and when he speaks them, three pyramids will rise at Giza, and they will stand forever. However, if he does not speak the magic words, everything that you, your son and your son's son have built will simply crumble away. It will turn into desert sand.'

'Then I decree,' said Khufu immediately, 'that all of the children of Rud-didet shall live in the greatest honour at Heliopolis. Should anyone, even a prince of Egypt, ever raise so much as a finger against any of these children, he will die the most shameful death. In addition, his body, which houses his Ka, or spirit, will also be completely destroyed. Hordedef, take Teta, the magician,' he commanded his son, 'to dwell with you in your palace for the rest of his days. Make sure that he receives a side of beef, five hundred cakes of bread, a hundred draughts of beer and anything else that he desires each day for the rest of his life.' Prince Hordedef obeyed his father.

Rud-didet's three children were born as Teta had predicted. One day, the eldest child, User-kaf, was playing in the temple of Amen-Ra when he discovered the flint casket that contained the papyrus roll on which

were written the magic words of power. He became a young priest and read the words from the papyrus when the Great Pyramid of Khufu was dedicated. When he became a high priest, he read the magic words of protection at the dedication of the pyramid of Khafra. And many years later, when he became pharaoh-elect, he read them again at the dedication of the pyramid of Menkaura.

When Menkaura died and was laid to rest in his pyramid, User-kaf became the first pharaoh of the Fifth Dynasty, just as Teta, the magician, had predicted. And the charm against Seth, the evil one, and the magic power of the words that he read have done everything that Khufu wanted them to do. To this day, the three great pyramids of Khufu, Khafra and Menkaura stand at Giza. They were the first of the Seven Wonders of the ancient world and, nearly five thousand years later, are the only ones that still remain.

103

'The Book of Thoth'

Setna, the son of Pharaoh Rameses the Great, was a magician. He was only interested in the ancient writings of Egypt and, unlike the other princes, had no time to lead his father's armies in guarding distant parts of the empire or to take part in hunts.

He was a scribe who could read and write the oldest of the hieroglyphs found on the walls of the temples – the many hundreds of signs that made up the language of the ancient Egyptians were quickly and easily recognised by Setna. And his magical arts were unsurpassed. Setna had learned his art of magic from the most secret of all of the ancient writings. Not even the priests of Thoth, Amen-Ra or Ptah could equal his skills.

Setna was poring over an ancient book written on two sides of a long roll

of papyrus one day when he came across the story of another pharaoh's son. Several hundred years earlier, this prince had also been a wise magician and great scribe. In fact, he had been even wiser and greater than Setna. This prince, whose name was Nefrekeptah, had read the Book of Thoth, which contained the language of the beasts and birds and all of the secrets of heaven and Earth.

As he read the papyrus, Setna learned that the Book of Thoth had been buried with Nefrekeptah in the royal tomb at Memphis. He immediately decided that he would not rest until he had found the book and had discovered all of its secrets for himself. 'Help me find the Book of Thoth', he begged his brother, Anheru, 'because without it my life has no further meaning.' 'Yes. We will go together', replied Anheru willingly.

So the two brothers set off for Memphis, where they found the tomb of Nefrekeptah, who, when he had lived three hundred years earlier, had been the son of a great pharaoh, Amen-hotep I.

Making their way into the tomb, Setna and his brother found the central chamber where the body of Nefrekeptah, wrapped in linen bands, was lying in a stone sarcophagus. Beside the sarcophagus, they were surprised to see the figures of a beautiful young woman and a young boy. The Book of Thoth lay between them, on the breast of the dead magician.

Bowing to the two figures with great reverence, Setna addressed them, saying, 'May Osiris have you in his keeping, Nefrekeptah, great scribe, dead son of a dead pharaoh, and you who sit beside him, whoever you may be! I am Setna, son of Rameses, who is the greatest pharaoh of all. I have come for the Book of Thoth, which, in your days on Earth, belonged to you. Let me, I beg you, take it in peace. If you do not, I am powerful enough to take it from you by magic or by force.'

'Setna, son of the pharaoh, I warn you, do not take the Book of Thoth! It will bring great trouble upon you,' replied the woman, 'just as it brought trouble to Nefrekeptah, who is lying here, and to me, his wife, and to his son.' 'Listen carefully to my story', she continued.

'My name is Ahura. Nefrekeptah and I were the children of Amen-hotep, the pharaoh many years ago. According to our custom, we became man and wife, and our son, Merab, was born. Nefrekeptah loved magic above everything else, and the ancient wisdom that can be learned from the carvings on temple walls and inside the tombs and pyramids of the priests and kings of Saqqara, who are long dead. Here, on the edge of Memphis, Saqqara is called the "City of the Dead"'.

'One day, as he was studying the carvings on the walls in an ancient shrine of the gods, Nefrekeptah heard the mocking laugh of a priest. "Everything that you are reading here is utterly worthless, but I could tell you the whereabouts of the Book of Thoth, which was written by the god of wisdom himself. After you have read only the first page, you will discover how to enchant not only heaven and Earth, but also the mountains, seas and abysses. You will learn the language of the birds, the reptiles and the beasts. By the time you have read the second page, you will have discovered all of the secrets of the gods and everything that is hidden in the stars."

"Tell me, then," replied Nefrekeptah, "what you want me to do for you. Whatever it is, I will do it if you will just tell me where the Book of Thoth can be found." "If you really want to know," said the priest, "you must give me one hundred bars of silver to pay for my funeral and order that I shall be buried like a king when I die."

So Nefrekeptah obeyed the priest.

"The Book of Thoth," said the priest, as soon as he had the hundred bars of silver in his hands, "lies at Koptos, in the middle of the river Nile, in an iron box. Inside the iron box is a bronze box, and inside that is a sycamore box. Inside the sycamore box is an ebony-and-ivory box, which has a silver box inside it. Inside the silver box is a box made of gold, and inside this box is the Book of Thoth." "But", he continued, 'there are snakes and scorpions twisted all around the iron box, which is guarded by a serpent. No one can kill this serpent."

Having hastened home to tell me this, Nefrekeptah was beside himself with delight, but I was afraid that some evil would befall him. "Do not go to Koptos to find this book," I begged him, "because I am sure that it will bring trouble to you and to those you love", and I tried to prevent him from going.

Nothing would stop him, however. Pushing me away, he went to our royal father and told him what he had heard from the priest. "What do you want from me?" asked the pharaoh. "Command your servants to prepare the royal boat immediately," replied Nefrekeptah, "because I wish to take

my wife and son with me and to sail to Koptos so that I can start searching for the book."

It was all done as he wished and we sailed south, along the Nile, to Koptos, where the priests and priestesses of Isis hurried to welcome us. They took us to the temple of Isis and Horus, where Nefrekeptah sacrificed a goose and an ox and made a libation of some wine. Then we feasted with the priests and their wives.

Nefrekeptah left me and our son four days later. As we watched from a window, he walked down to the river, where he performed some magic. First, he built a magic hut and filled it with the figures of men and equipment. Having cast a spell to give life to the men, he then caused the hut to sink into the river. Next he filled the royal boat with sand before sending it out into the middle of the Nile. When it had reached the place below which the magic hut had come to rest, he commanded, with great power and magic in his voice, "Workmen, work for me where the Book of Thoth lies!"

Day and night they worked, without stopping. After three days, they reached the place where the Book of Thoth lay. At the command of Nefrekeptah, the men raised the book out of the river.

Snakes and scorpions twisted and twined all around the iron box, and inside the box was the serpent that could not die.

Nefrekeptah shouted some loud and terrible words of magic that made the creatures quite still and unable to move. Unharmed, he walked through the snakes and scorpions until he came to the serpent, which lay curled inside the iron box. Then the serpent that could not die reared up, ready for battle. There was no magic charm strong enough to keep it still, so Nefrekeptah rushed at it as he drew his sword, cutting off its head with a single blow. But the serpent was immediately whole again and ready to strike. Nefrekeptah struck it again, this time throwing its head far away, into the river. But as soon as he had done so, the head returned and joined its body, and the snake was ready to strike for a third time.

By now, Nefrekeptah had realised that he could not kill the serpent and that he must overpower it with cunning instead. Again, he cut off its head, but this time he quickly covered each part of the serpent's body with sand, so that when the pieces tried to join themselves together again, they could not do so. The serpent that could not die lay helplessly in two pieces.

Watched by the snakes and the scorpions, and by the head of the serpent that could not die, Nefrekeptah approached the iron box, but none of them could hurt him. On opening the iron box, he found a bronze box with a sycamore box inside it. On opening that, he discovered a box of ebony and ivory, with a silver box inside it. At last he came to the golden box, inside which lay the Book of Thoth. And when he opened the book and began to read the first page, he immediately had power over the heavens and the Earth, the mountains, the seas and the abysses, and knew just what the birds, beasts and reptiles were saying. Then he read the second page, and when he read the magic spells written on it, he saw the moon and the stars, the sun shining in the sky and the gods who are hidden from sight, and he knew all of their secrets.

Nefrekeptah was satisfied that what the priest had told him had come true. And now the Book of Thoth belonged to him. Casting a magic spell on his workmen, he told them to take him back to Koptos, where I was sitting waiting for him. I had not moved since he left me, nor had I had anything to eat or drink. Nefrekeptah held out the Book of Thoth and I took it from him.

After I had read the first page, I also had the magical power that my husband had gained, and when I read the second, I knew all of the secrets of the gods.

Taking a fresh piece of papyrus, Nefrekeptah wrote down all of the spells in the Book of Thoth. Then he took a cup of beer, washed off the words written on the papyrus and drank the beer. Knowledge of the spells had now become part of him, but I could not write and was unable to remember all of the spells because many of them were so complicated.

Nefrekeptah, I and our son now began our return journey to Memphis on the royal boat. We had hardly set sail, when Merab, our little boy, was suddenly seized by something and was dragged into the river, disappearing from sight under the waters of the Nile. In panic, Nefrekeptah grabbed the Book of Thoth and began to read the necessary spell, whereupon Merab's body immediately returned to the surface and he was lifted back on board the royal boat. To our horror, however, all of the magic in the Book of Thoth was unable to bring our little boy back to life.

Then the spirit of our child spoke to Nefrekeptah, explaining what had caused his death. "The great god Thoth discovered that his precious book had been stolen. Hurrying to Amen-Ra, he said, 'The son of the Pharaoh Amen-hotep has found my magic box. He has immobilised the guards and taken the book that contains all of my magic.' Amen-Ra replied, 'Do whatever you think best to Nefrekeptah and

everything that is associated with him. Use my power to bring punishment and sadness to him, his wife and their child.' Ra's power thus drew me into the river Nile and drowned me."

We were heartbroken as we returned to Koptos, where we had our child's body embalmed and laid in a royal tomb. With the burial rites over, Nefrekeptah was anxious to return to Memphis as quickly as possible to tell our father what had happened. No sooner had we set sail again, than we reached the place where Merab had fallen into the water. Here the mighty power of Ra touched me, causing me to fall into the water and to drown. Once again Nefrekeptah had to return to Koptos, this time to bury his wife.

Finally, Nefrekeptah returned sadly to Memphis, but when the pharaoh went aboard the royal boat to greet his son, he discovered him lying dead in his cabin, with the precious Book of Thoth bound to his breast. All of the land of Egypt mourned for the pharaoh's son and his family, and Nefrekeptah was buried as custom dictated. He still lies in his tomb in Memphis, with his wife and son watching over him.'

Setna listened to Ahura's story in silence. Despite all that she had said, he still wanted the Book of Thoth with all of his heart. When he asked for it, Ahura and Merab drew back in fear. Then the spirit of Nefrekeptah suddenly spoke. 'If you will not heed the warning that my wife has given you, you must have the Book of Thoth! But you must win it. We will play a draughts contest, and if you beat me, the book is yours.' 'I am ready to play', replied Setna.

The contest began. Nefrekeptah won the first game and put a spell on Setna to make him sink into the ground to his ankles. When he won the second game, Setna sank into the ground to his waist. After the next game, only Setna's head was visible, and he called out to his brother, who was waiting outside the tomb. 'Go quickly and beg our father, the pharaoh, to give you the amulet of Ptah. It is the only thing that can save me. You must put it on my head before I play and lose the last game.'

Anheru fetched the amulet of Ptah as he was asked and hurried back to the tomb. As he entered, Setna was about to make his final move, while Nefrekeptah waited to win the game. Before Setna could move his piece, however, Anheru placed the amulet of Ptah on his brother's head. Setna immediately leapt out of the ground and snatched the Book of Thoth, the brothers then fleeing together from the tomb.

'Alas!' cried Ahura, 'He who lies here has lost all of his power.' 'Do not be sad,' replied the spirit of Nefrekeptah, 'Setna will be forced to return the book.' And then the tomb closed.

Setna returned to his father, gave him back the amulet of Ptah and told him what had happened. 'Take the Book of Thoth back to the tomb, my son,' his father advised him, 'for if you keep it, evil and sorrow will befall you for certain.' But Setna refused to listen to his father and kept the book, which he studied carefully for many years.

One day, while Setna was sitting under a shady colonnade in the temple of Ptah, a beautiful girl called Tabubua, wearing a golden headdress decorated with coloured jewels, entered the temple attended by fifty-two girls. Tabubua's mother was the cat goddess Bastet, from a city north of Memphis, and as Tabubua knelt before the statue of Ptah to make her offerings, Setna felt as though the goddess of love had cast a spell over him and he forgot everything, even the Book of Thoth.

Now all that Setna could think about was winning Tabubua for his own. He sent her a secret message, and her reply was that he could come in secret to visit her in her palace. Setna quickly made his way to her garden to meet her, and she led him to a private chamber, where she offered him a golden cup full of wine.

'I love you', he told her. 'And I,' she replied, with the sweetest smile, 'am destined to be your bride. But you must remember that I am no ordinary woman: my mother is Bastet the Beautiful. First you must prove to me that you have divorced your present wife and must promise that you will give me your children so that I can have them killed.' 'Whatever you wish', replied Setna, and promised her what she had demanded.

Draining the golden cup of wine, Setna turned to Tabubua, the woman who had so infatuated him, and told her, 'Now I have nothing left in the whole world. My wife is a beggar and all of my children are dead. Come to me, because I adore you.' With her arms outstretched, Tabubua came to him, but as soon as Setna embraced her, she suddenly faded and changed into a hideous corpse. Swirling darkness surrounded the terrified Setna, and when he regained consciousness he discovered that he was lying in the desert, completely naked.

The passers-by who saw him just laughed at Setna and went on their way, but one man, who was kinder than the others, threw him a shabby old coat. And so it was that Setna made his way back

to Memphis looking like a beggar.

On returning home, Setna found his wife and children alive and well. Realising that he must have been dreaming, he immediately decided to take the Book of Thoth back to Nefrekeptah. 'I have seen what terrible danger I am in,' he told his father, 'because if another spell like that is cast on me, next time it will not be a dream.' 'Yes,' replied Rameses, 'you have made the right decision.'

When he arrived at Nefrekeptah's tomb, Setna recited a spell and the door opened. 'What did I tell you?' asked Nefrekeptah, laughing. 'I told you that you would return the Book of Thoth to me. But don't imagine that you are free, because if you do not obey me now, the dream

of Tabubua will turn into reality.'

'What must I do?' asked Setna. 'One small thing', replied Nefrekeptah. 'As you know, my body rests here for you to see. Bring the bodies of Ahura and Mehab, which are resting in their tomb at Koptos, here. When the Day of Awakening comes, I wish them to be here with me.'

Returning to his father, Setna begged the pharaoh for the royal boat and, having won his agreement, sailed along the Nile to Koptos, where he made a sacrifice to Isis and Horus. Then, having found no record of where Ahura and Merab were buried, the despairing Setna offered a reward to anyone who could help him. An old man eventually tottered up to the temple and said, 'If

113

you are the great scribe, Setna, you must come with me. When I was a child, my grandfather showed me where Ahura and Merab were buried.'

The delighted Setna followed the old man to a house on the outskirts of Koptos. 'Pull down the house,' said the old man, 'and dig underneath it.' On doing as he was told, Setna came to a tomb buried under the sand. Inside lay the bodies of Ahura and Merab.

Setna returned to Memphis with the bodies and the pharaoh led a funeral procession, the culmination of which was the laying of the two bodies next to Nefrekeptah in his tomb, together with the Book of Thoth. Saying a final charm, Setna left the tomb as the door closed behind him. No trace of the door remained. Having heaped sand over the stone shrine near the once-visible entrance, the funeral party returned to the palace.

A sandstorm soon piled the sand into a huge mound, and when it levelled out there was no trace of the tomb. The Book of Thoth remains hidden forever – or at least until the Day of Awakening, when Osiris will return to rule the Earth.

114

'Se-Osiris and the Sealed Letter'

Setna, the wisest of all scribes and son of Rameses the Great, was famous in ancient Egypt. And by the age of twelve, Setna's son, Se-Osiris, had become the greatest magician that Egypt had ever known, as this story tells.

One day, Rameses was sitting in the great hall of his palace surrounded by his nobles and princes. Suddenly, the grand vizier, looking shocked, hurried into the hall with the news that a seven-foot-tall Ethiopian was demanding to see the pharaoh. 'He claims,' said the grand vizier, 'that he can prove that compared to the magic of Ethiopia, the magic of Egypt is nothing.' 'Let him come in', replied Rameses.

An enormous Ethiopian strode into the presence of the pharaoh. Bowing deeply, he addressed Rameses. 'King of all Egypt!' he said, 'Here in my hand I have brought you a sealed letter. Can any of your wonderful priests, scribes or magicians read what is written in it without breaking open the seal? If not, I will return to Ethiopia to tell my king

how weak Egyptian magic is, and you will be a laughing stock everywhere.'

When he heard this challenge, Rameses was both troubled and angry. He immediately sent for Setna, his wise son. When Setna heard what his father had to say, he was surprised and unhappy. 'Tell this barbarian to go to the royal guest house', he advised. 'He can eat, drink and sleep there until you reassemble your court. Then I will bring a magician who will show him that the practice of magic in Egypt is a match for anyone.'

The pharaoh agreed, and the Ethiopian was led away. Although Setna had spoken with great confidence, he was actually worried. He had read the Book of Thoth. He was the wisest man in the whole of Egypt. He knew that he was the most skilled of magicians. But he was certain that he could never read a letter that was written on a papyrus scroll that had then been rolled up and sealed without opening it.

Returning home, Setna lay down. He needed to think. Seeing how worried he was looking, his wife was afraid that he might be ill. When his son, Se-Osiris, came to see him, Setna told the boy what was worrying him. Laughing, the child replied, 'Father, you really have no need to worry. This is a gift from the gods that will bring glory to Egypt and make this overbearing king of Ethiopia and his wizards look foolish. Do not worry. I will read this sealed letter.'

Setna was amazed by the words of his small son, who looked, and sounded, so confident. 'I know that you have great magical powers, but how can I be sure that you can really read this sealed letter?' he asked his son. 'If you go to your room,' replied Se-Osiris, 'select any papyrus and then seal it carefully, I will show you that I can read it to you without you even giving it to me.'

Having preparing a papyrus according to the boy's instructions, Setna returned to his son. And while his father held the sealed papyrus roll in his hand, Se-Osiris read it perfectly.

When the pharaoh summoned his court again the next day, and everyone was assembled, the grand vizier was ordered to bring in the Ethiopian.

Appearing before the pharaoh, the enormous wizard held up his papyrus roll. 'King of all Egypt!' he said. 'Allow your magicians to read this. If they cannot, you must admit that our Ethiopian magic is greater than yours.'

Rameses turned to Setna and asked him, as the greatest magician in Egypt, to rise to the challenge. Bowing to his father, Setna replied, 'I would not insult a great Egyptian magician by asking him to bother himself with this challenge. Se-Osiris, my twelve-year-old son, has enough skill to read the letter.'

A murmur of amazement rippled through the assembled court and, as the small boy stepped forward, everyone

laughed. As the child approached the Ethiopian, who towered over him, scowling ferociously and holding the letter in his massive hand, the boy spoke in a clear voice. 'Grandfather, this letter, which is rolled up and sealed, contains a story about an insult. It is about a king of Ethiopia, who ruled five hundred years ago. He was sitting in his summerhouse beside the Nile, to the south of Egypt, one day. Behind him, sitting in the shade of a thick hedge, sat Ethiopia's greatest magicians, talking among themselves. The king could not help but overhear their conversation: each was trying to outdo the other with their bragging about the awful plagues that they could bring upon Egypt if they wanted to.

Summoning his magicians, the king told them that he had overheard them. "If you can do what you have boasted about," he told them, "I will give you the biggest reward that you can imagine." One of the magicians, Tnahsit, immediately began casting spells. He created a litter and four bearers from wax; chanting magical words, he breathed life into the men and commanded them to go to Egypt that night to bring the pharaoh to Ethiopia.'

Rameses then turned to the Ethiopian. 'Tell me the truth. Are the words that the boy has spoken those that are written in the sealed letter that you are holding?' 'Indeed they are', replied the Ethiopian, bowing low before the pharaoh.

As Se-Osiris continued reading the letter, he revealed that everything that had been threatened by the king of Ethiopia had happened: the pharaoh had been taken to Ethiopia, where he had been beaten in public. On his return to Thebes, the marks on his back proved that he had not been dreaming. His shame had provoked him to take vengeance against the king of Ethiopia and his magicians.

'How,' he had asked Kherheb, his chief magician, 'can I ensure the future safety of Egypt and the pharaohs?' 'Tonight I shall go to the great temple of Thoth, the god of wisdom and magic, who will certainly give me a charm to protect you and bring vengeance upon the Nubians and the Ethiopians', the magician had confidently replied.

Thoth, the god with the head of an ibis, gave the magician certain instructions, and when the Ethiopian litter-bearers returned to the palace to kidnap the pharaoh for a second time, they encountered a magic so strong that they just stood and gibbered. Unable to complete their task, they disappeared, and were never seen again in Egypt.

Satisfying his master's desire for revenge, Kherheb kidnapped the king of Ethiopia and carried him to Thebes. The king was beaten in the square in front of the temple of Amen-Ra, where a crowd had gathered, before being returned to his palace with the marks on his back bearing testimony to his punishment. The king of Ethiopia, who was both in pain and very angry, sent for his magicians and commanded them to protect him against the Egyptian magicians. Nothing worked against the power of the pharaoh,

however, and he was taken to Thebes on two further occasions, where the beatings were repeated. Eventually the king of Ethiopia was forced to humble himself before the great god, while the son of Tnahsit was banished to wander the Earth until he had found a way of producing magic greater than that of the Egyptians.

This was the story that was told within the sealed letter, as the Ethiopian was forced to admit before the seal was broken and the letter read out to the pharaoh's court. Se-Osiris, this amazing child, had known all of it before the seal was broken.

Bowing low, the Ethiopian cringed before the pharaoh, pleading, 'May I now go back to my home?' Se-Osiris quickly told the pharaoh who the Ethiopian really was, because, of course, he was the son of Tnahsit, who was trying to wreak his magical revenge on the Egyptians. 'We should surely finish this old battle of magic between Egypt and Ethiopia now', Se-Osiris advised the pharaoh, and Rameses agreed. 'I command you today to finish what was begun five hundred years ago', Rameses told Se-Osiris. 'As for you,' he thundered at the Ethiopian, 'now match your magic of the south against the magic of Egypt.'

Waving the sealed letter like a wand, the Ethiopian cursed and muttered his most powerful magic, directing it at the pharaoh. Hissing loudly, an evil serpent suddenly appeared, baring its poisoned fangs and flickering its forked tongue. The terrified pharaoh cowered behind his courtiers, but Se-Osiris just laughed, lifted his hand and picked up the snake, which shrank into a tiny, white worm before being thrown out of the window by the child.

Giving a howl of rage, the Ethiopian spat out curses and muttered magic incantations, causing a dark cloud to envelope the hall until it was like a black tomb at midnight. Laughing as he did so, Se-Osiris crushed the darkness into a tiny ball and threw it out of the window to join the snake.

Again the Ethiopian shouted and waved his arms, as if he were possessed. This time, an enormous sheet of fire appeared and began to move towards the pharaoh sitting on his royal throne. Laughing again, Se-Osiris blew on the fire, which shrank back and wrapped itself right around the Ethiopian magician. As the Ethiopian gave a last, piercing cry, the flame disappeared like a blown-out candle, leaving a little pile of ash on the floor in front of Rameses.

'Son of Tnahsit,' said Se-Osiris, 'farewell! You will never insult the pharaoh of Egypt again or threaten the land of Egypt with your evil magic.' And it was so.

Egyptian hieroglyphs

The language of the ancient Egyptians boasts nearly five thousand more years of recorded history than any other language, making it one of the oldest in the world. It was spoken from around **4000 BC** until the eleventh century AD, after which it expired as a spoken tongue and was replaced by Arabic during the Middle Ages. Although the language of the ancient Egyptians is today a dead language, it is still used in a fossilised form by the Christian Coptic Church in Egypt.

Written scripts

The three scripts that were used in ancient Egypt for writing the Egyptian language were the hieroglyphic, hieratic and demotic. The earliest script, which dated from about 3100 BC to AD 400, was hieroglyphic, whose recognisable forms represented a person, an idea or an object. These symbols could be combined with different signs, which was how the words of the spoken language were spelled. Only consonants were indicated in the hieroglyphs, which were used for formal inscriptions, of which remnants have been found on ivory, pottery and stone artefacts.

The hieroglyphic script was pictorial, identifying it with ancient Egyptian culture. Yet the hieroglyphs were not a form of primitive writing, but formed a completely developed system that communicated complex information.

Over time, the script evolved, with new signs being added to the language. (About seven hundred hieroglyphs were in use during the Old Kingdom, for example, but by the time of the Ptolemaic period there were more than six thousand.)

The hieroglyphic script was flexible and was written both in horizontal rows and vertical columns. The direction of the signs could be changed, so that they could be written from left to right, as well as from right to left (the ancient Egyptians generally never wrote from bottom to top). The aesthetic appearance of the text was the most important factor in placing the signs, and because empty spaces were discouraged, texts were arranged in squares.

The hieratic script was a more simplified style of writing than the hieroglyphic script that was used at the same time,

until about 650 BC. An adaptation of the hieroglyphic script, it was a quicker method of recording that was used for business and administrative purposes, as well as for writing religious, scientific and literary documents. The earliest hieratic writing is more fluent than the hieroglyphic script, but by the time of the Old Kingdom its individual signs had become much more abbreviated. Hieratic inscriptions were mostly made with a reed brush and black ink.

The demotic script, which was used between 650 BC and AD 450, was another simplified method of writing that was distinct from the hieratic script, having its own, independent form. Written in horizontal lines, the script was cursive and included no pictures or icons.

The use of traditional scripts gradually declined in ancient Egypt early in the Christian period, eventually disappearing altogether. Because Egyptian Christians spoke Coptic, the Coptic script represented the beginning of the final phase of the original Egyptian language. Coptic script borrowed heavily from various Semitic languages and Greek. The alphabet consisted of twenty-four letters of the Greek alphabet, each of which represented a single sound, while six signs from the demotic alphabet were adapted from the sounds that were not represented in Greek. Coptic became a fully alphabetical script, with both vowels and consonants being represented.

The Egyptian alphabet

It was the discovery of the Rosetta Stone in 1799, by Napoleonic troops fighting in Egypt, that made it possible to decipher ancient Egyptian writing. Although the French claimed the stone first, the British, who had won a skirmish against the French, demanded it, and it eventually ended up in the British Museum, in London, where it can be seen today.

The Rosetta Stone is written in three languages. At the top, much of the writing has been broken off; this part is written in the Egyptian hieroglyphic script. The central text is written in the Egyptian demotic script, while the text at the bottom of the stone is written in Koine Greek, a dialect that was used in Egypt during the Hellenistic period, from 323 to 31 BC. The text represented in the three sections is identical, and because the nineteenth-century Egyptologists who studied the Rosetta Stone were familiar with both Koine Greek and demotic Egyptian, they were able to decipher the meaning of the Egyptian hieroglyphic script.

Hieroglyphic magic: the Egyptian oracle

The ancient Egyptians believed that hieroglyphs possessed magical meanings. In spiritual terms, blessings came to both rich and poor in the afterlife; magical concepts were connected with spirituality, and hieroglyphic symbols were believed to contain spiritual energies that were released whenever they were spoken or written.

One way for us to harness the ancient magic of the Egyptians is to use hieroglyphic cards: triggering an inner power, which is focused on the meaning of each sacred symbol, is a method of understanding the dilemmas of modern, everyday life.

During a reading, it may be helpful to surround yourself with some of the crystals – richly gleaming stones that give out warmth and light (see box) – that are traditionally associated with ancient Egyptian amulets and hieroglyphs. For further inspiration, you could light some candles: golden candles to symbolise the sun, and brown candles to represent the mud of the life-giving river Nile.

The symbolic significance of crystals and metals in Egyptian magic.

Stone or metal	Colour	Symbol
Lapis lazuli	Deep blue, flecked with gold	Heart
Fossilised wood	Brown	Ladder
Carnelian	Orange	The sun
Haematite	Silvery grey	Pillow
Quartz	Clear	The eye of Horus
Jasper	Yellow or red	The ankh
Gold	Gold	Isis or Ra
Silver	Silver	Osiris

Making oracle cards

Either photocopy the hieroglyphs illustrated below or draw them on a large piece of stiff card, which should be either white or yellow and about twice the size of the illustrations. Now cut up the card to form fifteen oracle cards, which should be slightly larger than normal playing cards. Leave the reverse side blank.

How to do a reading

Shuffle or mix the cards and place them face down.

Arrange them in a circle.

Select the 3rd, 7th and 9th cards. These are the most magical positions.

Repeat this to give you the past situation, the present and the future possible outcome.

These cards will give you the three steps you will need to take to succeed or the three best principles which will guide you for your immediate situation or decision.

Remember that the symbol on each card was worn as an amulet for power or protection. It was always set in precious metals or jewels.

The symbols offered growth and strength for the living and, on amulets or tomb walls, the promise of resurrection for those who had died.

Tradition has it that the cards should not be consulted more than once a week. However, if you have an especially difficult or important week you might wish to use the cards more than once. Remember that three cards are probably the most that will be of use at any one reading unless the same card appears twice. Any duplicate suggests that you may expect almost immediate results from the reading.

As you become familiar with the cards you may find that you give your own interpretations which fit better. Write them down in a book, which you should keep specially for your Oracle card readings.

Remember that if you are ever in any doubt you should always allow your intuition to guide you to your answer.

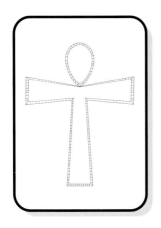

1. The ankh

Significance: the ankh, or the key, is the Egyptian symbol of eternal life. In tomb wall paintings, it is depicted being held to the nose of a pharaoh to ensure his continuing life after death (this indicates that the ancient Egyptians believed that the nose was the source of life).

Meaning: in a reading, the ankh represents all that is both of great worth and enduring. Any current relationship or situation is worth fighting for, and persisting, despite any doubts or difficulties, is advised.

Message: the message of the ankh is to seek what is of lasting worth and to persevere.

2. Wedja

Significance: the ancient Egyptians used fire to forge metal, with gold being smelted to create beautiful pieces of jewellery. This hieroglyph represents the bow drill, which was turned in a piece of shaped wood to produce friction and fire. Wedja is the symbol for prosperity, as well as the means by which money can be made or material security achieved.

Meaning: in a reading, wedja is concerned with material affairs and the importance of considering the financial implications of any decision. It warns against risk-taking.

Message: try to resolve any money worries rather than doing nothing and hoping that they will go away. Prudence and consolidation are advised.

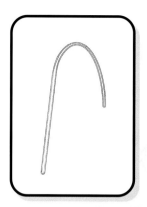

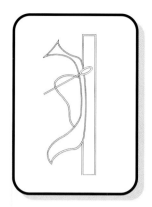

3. Seneb

Significance: the first letter in the word seneb, this hieroglyph symbolises health. The concept of health and well-being was incorporated in pharaohs' tombs by means of three signs – ankh, wedja and seneb – written after the pharaoh's name, which was believed to ensure eternal life, prosperity and health in the world to come.

Meaning: in a reading, the appearance of this symbol indicates that health matters are of importance. You may be feeling stressed or anxious, and it is likely that this will affect you, both physically and mentally.

Message: the message is to take care of yourself. Avoid people who make you feel inadequate, turn your back on conflict and take charge of your own health and well-being in a positive manner.

4. Boat

Significance: because the river Nile was central to their lives, the boat was the main means of transportation for the ancient Egyptians. The boat was not only important to mortals, however, for each day the sun god, Ra, crossed the sky in his solar boat.

Meaning: the hieroglyph of the boat represents the overcoming of obstacles and the attainment of goals. Whenever the boat appears in a reading, it may indicate that the qualities of resourcefulness and adaptability are required with which to use any means to attain a goal. The promise of the boat is that those who are prepared to consider looking beyond their immediate circumstances for a solution will find a way to ensure their success.

Message: the message of the boat is to expand all possibilities and to be adaptable.

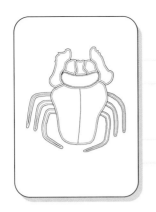

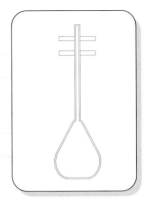

5. Scarab

Significance: the beetle that lays its eggs in a small ball of nourishing dung was a profound symbol of rebirth for the ancient Egyptians, who believed that the young beetles that emerged from the ball of dung represented transformation and rebirth.

Meaning: in a reading, the scarab again represents transformation and rebirth. If difficulties or problems have closed certain doors, it promises future success and happiness.

Message: remember that tomorrow is another day, and that the seeds of happiness and success lie within each of us. However dark it may seem, when the scarab appears, there is always the chance of a new beginning.

6. Nefer

Significance: this is the symbol of a musical instrument that resembled a primitive guitar. The instrument was thought to produce a perfect blend of form and harmony and therefore represented pleasure and fulfilment. The meaning of this hieroglyph is accordingly one of happiness, beauty and good fortune.

Meaning: whenever this symbol appears in a reading, it indicates that the main concern is your own happiness. It does not matter if the source of your happiness is not what others consider to be worldly success. This symbol urges you to let your inner joy shine through and to concentrate on creating your own harmony.

Message: the message of Nefer is to find something positive to rejoice in each day, however hard it seems, or however difficult your circumstances.

7. Tet

Significance: this symbol represents the tree trunk within which Isis hid Osiris' dead body. It also denotes the backbone of Osiris, the essential element required for the reforming of his body. At the festivals of Osiris, the tet was ceremonially raised into an upright position to signify a source of stability (a quality that the ancient Egyptians prized very highly) and strength.

Meaning: in a reading, tet represents the firm foundations and stability that are essential for the success of any venture.

Message: tet's message is that any plans for work ventures or relationships are well rooted, and that with endurance and patience, they will come to fruition. Tet tells us not to waver before opposition, but to stand firm instead.

8. Pillow

Significance: in ancient Egypt, the head of a mummy was always supported by a pillow, which both protected and raised it in its coffin. This symbol represents the spiritual sense of the raising of the immortal soul to ensure its triumph over the death of the body.

Meaning: in a reading, the pillow symbolises the seeking of support in overcoming difficulties and, rather than trying to succeed alone, tells us to enlist the encouragement and help of others in trying to achieve a chosen goal.

Message: if you are experiencing difficulties, the impetus to succeed will come from sympathetic support, so when trying to achieve a positive aim, do not stand alone, but always seek the help of others.

9. Heart

Significance: as the seat of life, the ancient Egyptians regarded the heart as the source of both good and evil thoughts. After death, the heart required very special protection, and the symbol of the heart is the urn that was used to preserve it, separately from the body. In the afterlife, the heart was weighed in a balance against a symbolic feather representing truth and right.

Meaning: principles and ideals are symbolised when the heart appears in a reading – perhaps they are under threat or are in danger of being compromised. The dilemma here concerns what is really important for the sake of love or peace.

Message: the heart's message is that you will be guided by your principles because you will know in your own heart the right path to take. Be true to yourself and to your core beliefs.

10. The Eye of Horus

Significance: this powerful symbol represents the white or sun's 'eye' that can be seen when the summer solstice (the longest day of the year) is at its height. Although the ancient Egyptians did not hold festivals to mark the solstices, the sun was the most vital element for life and growth in ancient Egypt, and in magical terms the sun also had great power. The full power of the sun is represented by the eye of Horus. Left-brain energy (traditionally the intellectual side associated with the sun) is assertive, illuminating every corner of the being with power and light and casts away all doubt and inertia.

Meaning: the appearance of the eye of Horus in a reading indicates the desire and strength to succeed.

Message: the message of the eye of Horus is to make a supreme effort to succeed in your chosen path. Whatever you choose to do, have confidence in your power and ability.

11. Menat

Significance: this symbol represents fertility, nourishment and reproduction through the coming-together of male and female energy. Its fertility aspect not only denotes human fertility, but also the fertility of the river Nile, which floods annually.

Meaning: abundance, increase and giving are symbolised by menat, so whenever it appears in a reading, it indicates that you should be concerned with giving. Give of yourself freely to those close to you, who will benefit from your love and your time. In this sense, menat represents generosity of action and spirit.

Message: menat's message is the more open and generous your approach to life, the more you will receive in return.

12. Vulture

Significance: the vulture, which has an ankh of life engraved on each talon, is the symbol of Isis, the divine mother, and represents power and protection of the deceased. When his evil uncle, Seth, planned to destroy him, Isis cared for Horus in the marshes, demonstrating her great powers of maternal protection.

Meaning: when the vulture appears in a reading, it denotes that it is time to care for and nurture others whenever they are vulnerable. Caring for others is a creative power that gives both great satisfaction and the opportunity for personal growth.

Message: the message of the vulture is to nurture and protect those who are close to you when they are in need.

Egyptian hieroglyphs

13. Collar of Gold

Significance: on the day of the funeral, a collar of gold was placed around a deceased ancient Egyptian's neck to allow the soul to escape from the earthly bindings wrapping the body.

Meaning: because this symbol represents independence from those who attempt to stifle identity, as well as from any need for material security, when the collar of gold appears in a reading, it may be a sign that you have become too involved in the needs and problems of others. Your life may be suffering through your inattention to your own needs, so perhaps you should be more assertive and should establish your own identity.

Message: the collar of gold urges you to take your first step towards independence, be it in your personal life or at work. Accord your own identity and needs a more prominent position within your life.

14. Ladder

Significance: it was believed that the dead could gain access to the heavens by using a ladder. (Ancient Egyptians believed the floor of the heavens was a rectangular, iron plate, supported by four iron pillars, where the dead lived with the gods.) Ra created the ladder to enable his son, Osiris, to ascend to heaven, and the symbol of the ladder indicates a transition from the material world to a higher level of awareness, allowing access to the realm of unconscious spiritual wisdom.

Meaning: the ladder is telling you to place your trust in inspiration and intuition and to refuse to listen to the voice of logic or to others' advice. Follow your dreams, however insignificant, and listen carefully to the voice of wisdom coming from deep within your spirit.

Message: the message of the ladder is to follow your visions and dreams and to listen to your inner voice.

15. Shen

Significance: shen was an ancient Egyptian symbol of time, representing the orbit of the sun around the Earth. A shen amulet was placed upon the dead to represent the enduring power of the sun and the promise of eternal life.

Meaning: when shen appears in a reading, it is telling you that it is important to move forwards in your life.

Message: the message of shen in a reading is clear: do not wait for a perfect opportunity to come in the future, but seize the moment and act now because time does not wait.

PART FOUR

Egyptian birth signs and astrology

Many people are drawn to the exotic spirituality of ancient Egypt and then become fascinated by the deities who govern the months of the year, each of which have an associated essence that could be called the 'flavour of the month'. (Having their origins in the reign of Pharaoh Akhenaton, such flowers, herbs and stones were all used in the ancient system of Egyptian magic.) These mysterious and fascinating ancient gods, with their bizarre appearances, can still inspire the imagination today.

- Sekhmet was the lioness-headed goddess of fire and power, who gave strength.

- Hathor, most often represented as a beautiful woman, but sometimes as a cow, had a lusty joy of life and was the goddess of love.

- Anubis, with his jackal's head, was the weigher of hearts.

- Thoth, with his ibis' head, represented wisdom and writing.

Four thousand years ago, the ancient Egyptians developed their own system of birth signs, depictions of which were discovered in the Temple of the Sun by archaeologists, showing that mystical Egyptian horoscopes were divided into twelve signs, each ruled by a different god. (See pages 140 to 151 for details of the deities that ruled the months of the year, together with their associations.)

We know very little about ancient Egyptian astrology, however, and only one astrological design has survived, in the form of a stone disc measuring 12 inches (30.5 centimetres) in diameter, which was discovered on the ceiling of the Temple of Hathor, at Dendera in central Egypt, and which today can be seen in the Louvre, in Paris. This disc was probably made at around the end of the period known as the New Kingdom, which includes the reign of Cleopatra, and the era when the Romans annexed the kingdom of Egypt to their empire between 58 and 30 BC.

The Egyptians divided the zodiac into eighteen constellations, which were represented by animals, but these were not used for natal astrology. Each birth sign was instead determined by a month of the Egyptian year, and the birth signs on the decorated Dendera disc depict the creatures and deities attributed to each month, and hence birth sign. Inscriptions found at the Temple of Hathor tell us that the divinities were believed to influence the mental and physical characteristics of each individual born under the sign associated with them, although no information on hieroglyphic inscriptions exists to give us exact details about the individual characteristics of each sign.

Unlike our year, which comprises four seasons consisting of three months, the ancient Egyptian year was divided into three seasons consisting of four months. The three seasons were, firstly, the inundation, when the river Nile overflowed its banks and fertilised the rich, dark soil; secondly, the growing season, when the land was farmed; and, thirdly, the harvest season, when the crops were gathered, the weather was blisteringly hot and the land parched, bringing the cycle to an end (the Egyptian climate allowed for no winter season).

Between 2686 and 2181 BC in the Old Kingdom, the twelve months of the new year began on 21 March, the spring equinox. During the period of the Middle Kingdom, (2040–1782 BC) following several political upheavals, however, the heliacal rising of the star Sirius, (known as Sothis to the ancient Egyptians), which occurred in about the middle of July, heralded the start of the new year.

Yet belief systems varied throughout the country, and some areas continued to calculate their calendar according to the original system, in which the deities associated with each month also varied.

The early ancient Egyptian calendar followed a lunar cycle that became slightly out of alignment over the years. In order to correct this, five extra days were eventually added between what we now know as 14 to 18 July inclusive, in the same way as our leap year occurs every four years on 29

February. These extra days were considered to be holy days because they were said to be the birthdays of especially important gods, namely the children of the Earth god, Geb, and the sky goddess, Nut:

■ 14 July was the birthday of Osiris, the god of the underworld;

■ 15 July was the birthday of Horus the Elder, a falcon-headed god;

■ 16 July was the birthday of Seth, the god of chaos and evil;

■ 17 July was the birthday of Isis, who became the wife of Osiris and was believed to have great magical powers;

■ 18 July was the birthday of Nephthys, who married Seth and was said to have had a child with Osiris, who was known as Anubis, the jackal-headed god.

By the end of ancient Egyptian history, after several alterations to the date of the new year and the start of each month during different periods, the year was eventually deemed to begin on 29 August, with the inundation of the Nile. Following many changes, the calendar had been fully worked out, and this was when the Dendera zodiac was finally introduced.

Thoth, Lord of the Moon

29 August to 27 September

In the ancient Egyptian world, Thoth was sometimes known as Tehuti, but was always recognisable by his ibis head. The god of learning and imagination, who presided over knowledge and scribes, Thoth was the lord of time.

The following were associated with Thoth:

Stone	Carnelian
Colour	Bright orange
Number	Eight
Scent	Lavender
Creature	Ibis
Flower	Marigold
Tree	Quince
Herb	Thyme
Food	Orange

O great Thoth, lord of the mind and guardian of learning, you are the bringer of knowledge to humankind.

Horus, God of the rising sun

28 September to 27 October

Horus, the falcon-headed son of Osiris and Isis, was the symbol of divine
kingship and the god of the rising sun. To avenge his father's death, he risked
his life to oppose Seth, his father's slayer, losing an eye during the battle,
which became the ultimate talisman of protection, a precious stone
that symbolised eternal life and resurrection.

The following were associated with Horus:

Stone	Citrine
Colour	Yellow-gold
Number	Six
Scent	Frankincense
Creature	Falcon
Flower	Carnation
Tree	Acacia
Herb	Rosemary
Food	Sunflower seeds

I am the lord of the morning sun. I am one who is with
the sound eye; even when closed, I am in its protection.

Wadjet, the Royal Cobra Goddess

28 October to 26 November

Legend told that the royal cobra goddess of ancient Egypt, who was also
known as Uatchat, created the papyrus swamps of Delta. As a deity of kingship,
her image – a cobra poised to strike, called the uraeus – adorned the
front of the pharaoh's crown. Wadjet was the symbol of knowledge.

The following were associated with Wadjet:

Stone	Amethyst
Colour	Lilac
Number	Ten
Scent	Rose
Creature	Serpent
Flower	Hyacinth
Tree	Ash
Herb	Mustard
Food	Lemon

It is through the will of the great serpent
goddess that all kings shall rule.

Sekhmet, the Goddess of War and the Desert

27 November to 26 December

The fire-breathing, lioness-headed Sekhmet was the most feared of all of the Egyptian deities. The mistress of fire, she was known as the 'Eye of Ra', signifying the sun's intense heat. Sekhmet was also regarded as a deity of mystical power and a goddess of healing, whose priests were physicians.

The following were associated with Sekhmet:

Stone	Tiger's eye
Colour	Red
Number	Five
Scent	Red sandalwood
Creature	Lioness
Flower	Poppy
Tree	Sandalwood
Herb	Pepper
Food	Cinnamon

O mighty one, great of magic, wise and powerful daughter of Ra.

The Sphinx, the Shape-shifter

27 December to 25 January

Originally known as Hu, the sphinx was the most enigmatic of all of the Egyptian birth signs. A treasure guardian, the sphinx, which was able to change into the form of any other creature, symbolised mystical power.

The following were associated with the Sphinx:

Stone	Quartz
Colour	White
Number	One
Scent	Eucalyptus
Creature	Lion
Flower	Lily
Tree	Almond
Herb	Coriander
Food	White grapes

None can solve the riddle of the sphinx,
be he god or mortal man.

Shu, the God of Sunlight

26 January to 24 February

Shu was represented as a human being with an ostrich feather on his head, which was also his hieroglyphic sign. The god of sunlight and air, Shu was the brother and consort of Tefnut and was known as one of the divine twins.

The following were associated with Shu:

Stone	Moonstone
Colour	Purple
Number	Nine
Scent	White sandalwood
Creature	Swallow
Flower	Iris
Tree	Silver birch
Herb	Lemon balm
Food	Lychee

May the breath of Shu bring life
to the earth. May his passing
cleanse the sky.

Iris, the Goddess of Order

25 February to 26 March

Isis, the symbolic mother of the pharaoh, the sister and wife of Osiris and the mother of Horus, was known in ancient Egypt as Aset. Represented as a beautiful woman, Isis was worshipped as the 'Great of Magic'. She was the goddess of order, and her name meant 'throne' or 'seat'. Both practical and intuitive, Isis was able to see things from all points of view.

The following were associated with Iris:

Stone	Lapis lazuli
Colour	Green
Number	Seven
Scent	Lotus
Creature	Cat
Flower	Rose
Tree	Sycamore
Herb	Tarragon
Food	Avocado

Blood of Iris, bring forth the great magic
that will transform the world.

Osiris, the God of the Underworld

27 March to 25 April

Osiris was known as the 'Lord of the Nile' and the god of the underworld.
In ancient Egypt, his name was Asar, and he was represented in
human form, carrying the insignia of a ruler – the crook and flail –
across his chest. His sign is one of communication.

The following were associated with Osiris:

Stone	Moss agate
Colour	Silvery grey
Number	Two
Scent	Myrrh
Creature	Scarab
Flower	Violet
Tree	Cedar
Herb	Basil
Food	Pomegranate

Osiris, the eternally good, the perfect one, he who
sits in the place of the all-seeing eye.

Amun, the Supreme God of State

26 April to 25 May

During the Late Period of ancient Egypt, Amun became the supreme
state god. It was said that it was Amun who brought the cosmos into
existence and who created the Earth and sky from his thoughts.
Amun was sometimes pictured in completely human form,
but at other times he was depicted with the head of a ram.

The following were associated with Amun:

Stone	Turquoise
Colour	Blue
Number	Four
Scent	Cloves
Creature	Ram
Flower	Bluebell
Tree	Oak
Herb	Sage
Food	Damson

Amun, O hidden one,
he who abides in all things,
he who rules over all.

Hathor, the Goddess of the Land and Sky

26 May to 24 June

In ancient Egypt, Hathor was called Het-Het. Goddess of both the land and sky, Hathor had associations with love, music and dancing. Hathor was sometimes depicted as a white cow, while at other times she was portrayed in human form, wearing the sun disc on her head.

The following were associated with Hathor:

Stone	Jasper
Colour	Ochre
Number	Ten
Scent	Patchouli
Creature	Cow
Flower	Cowslip
Tree	Elm
Herb	Fennel
Food	Olive

In the following of Hathor, may I be inspired to create in her name.

The Phoenix, the symbol of Life and Rebirth

25 June to 24 July

Legend tells that this exotic bird made a nest of spices, and that when the rays of the sun set its nest alight, the phoenix was burnt to a cinder. After several days, however, a new phoenix was born and rose from the ashes. Called 'Benu', the phoenix was the ancient Egyptians' sacred firebird, a symbol of life and rebirth.

The following were associated with the Phoenix:

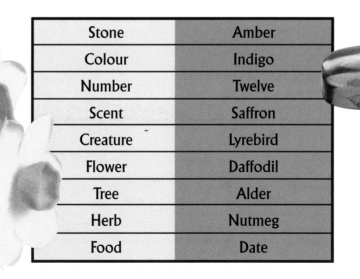

Stone	Amber
Colour	Indigo
Number	Twelve
Scent	Saffron
Creature	Lyrebird
Flower	Daffodil
Tree	Alder
Herb	Nutmeg
Food	Date

Lord of jubilees, I have gone forth as a phoenix, risen and shining

Anubis, the Judge of Souls and Guardian of the Underworld

25 July to 28 August

In ancient Egypt, Anpu, as Anubis was called, was considered the guardian of the underworld and the protector of souls.
Depicted with the head of a jackal, the energy of Anubis was protective.

The following were associated with Anubis:

Stone	Obsidian
Colour	Black
Number	Three
Scent	Chypre
Creature	Jackal
Flower	Foxglove
Tree	Yew
Herb	Savory
Food	Apple

Anubis, O lord of the hallowed land, weigh my
soul at the time of my crossing.

A felucca sailing boat on the Nile.

A timeline for ancient Egypt

The ancient Egyptian civilisation, which was based around the river Nile, emerged five thousand years ago and reached its peak in the sixteenth century BC. Ancient Egypt was famed for its great power and wealth, due to the highly fertile lands of the Nile delta, which were a rich source of grain for the whole Mediterranean region. The ancient Egyptians were advanced practitioners of agriculture, engineering and applied sciences, and many of their monuments, such as the pyramids and the Sphinx, still survive today.

The Egyptians lived by farming the banks of the Nile, growing corn, vegetables, date palms and grapevines; bread and beer were their staple food and drink. Experts in irrigation, they constructed canals, dykes and dams to increase the output of food crops. They also studied the seasons and calculated that a year contained 365 days. Trade was conducted by bartering – there was no coinage, and external trade was under the control of foreigners.

Surrounded as it was by deserts and seas, ancient Egypt developed in virtual isolation to become the world's first nation state. The king, or pharaoh, was regarded as a god, whose will was absolute. The kingdom was divided into administrative districts called nomes, each one being headed by a nomarch or governor. A hierarchy of nobles, priests and scribes supervised agriculture and trade.

Ancient Egyptian religion

Ra, the sun god, and Osiris, the god of the dead, were the chief deities of ancient Egypt, and many other gods were believed to control the processes of birth and death and various aspects of everyday life. The gods were depicted with the heads of the animals or birds that were sacred to them, for example:

- the hawk was sacred to Ra;

- the ibis was sacred to Thoth;

- the jackal was sacred to Anubis.

The local deity of Thebes, Amun, eventually became the supreme god as the 'Lord of the Thrones of the Two Lands', a symbol of national unity.

Although immortality was originally the preserve of the pharaohs, under the New Kingdom, almost all of those who could afford mummification – an essential prerequisite for immortality in

The massive temple of Karnak.

ancient Egyptian belief – achieved it. Most evidence of ancient Egyptian life derives from tombs, because the dead were usually buried with everything necessary to maintain their standard of living in the afterworld. The royal statues, jewellery, ornaments and furniture that have been found in ancient Egyptian tombs are of the finest quality, while the walls are painted with detailed scenes in distinctive, two-dimensional style, also being inscribed with extracts from various religious texts.

Ancient Egyptian language and literature

Although knowledge of the ancient Egyptian language was eventually lost, examples of ancient Egyptian script discovered by archaeologists have been deciphered as a result of the knowledge gained by studying the Rosetta Stone (see page 124).

Egyptian literature included mythological and historical tales, poetry and moral essays, two of the most famous surviving examples being 'The Story of the Shipwrecked Sailor' and 'The Tale of the Two Brothers'.

Ancient Egyptian architecture

The pyramids were the tombs of the pharaohs, and the shape of these enormous structures is almost certainly connected with the belief that the dead pharaoh ascended to the sky to merge with the sun god.

Egyptian architects built on the grandest scale. Having developed their knowledge of geometry and trigonometry for use in surveying, their earliest buildings, including the pyramids, were constructed of accurately positioned blocks of solid stone. Later on, such buildings as the temples of Luxor and Karnak at Thebes featured massive lintels supported by tall columns.

Ancient Egyptian history

Ancient Egyptian history is divided into thirty-one royal dynasties, usually grouped together under a name, as follows.

The Archaic period (First and Second dynasties)

Menes, the first pharaoh, united the Nile delta (Lower Egypt) with the Nile valley (Upper Egypt) to form one long, narrow kingdom, whose capital was at Memphis. The religion and administration of the new kingdom now took on the forms that later became established throughout Egypt.

The Old Kingdom (Third to Sixth dynasties inclusive)

The Step Pyramid at Saqqara was built by the architect Imhotep for Pharaoh Zoser. The pharaohs of the Fourth Dynasty constructed the pyramids of Giza/Ghiza, culminating in the massive Great Pyramid of Cheops commissioned by Pharaoh Cheops. At the end of the Sixth Dynasty, Pharaoh Pepi II reputedly reigned for nearly a century, but gradually lost control of the kingdom as the nomarchs increasingly became independent hereditary rulers.

The First Intermediate period
(Seventh to Tenth dynasties inclusive)

Amid civil war and famine, Egypt broke up into several minor kingdoms. After a century of disorder, the kingdom of Thebes began to reunite the country.

The Middle Kingdom (Eleventh and Twelfth dynasties)

Pharaoh Mentuhotep II completed the reunion of Egypt by suppressing the hereditary nomarchs. As a result, the kingdom began to expand and the arts were revived. During the Twelfth Dynasty, the oasis of Fayum, west of the Nile, was irrigated and eventually became the 'garden of Egypt'.

The Second Intermediate period
(Thirteenth to Seventeenth dynasties inclusive)

It was during the Second Intermediate period that Egypt suffered another dark age of anarchy, causing the country to disintegrate into chaos once again. The country was dominated for about a century by the Hyksös, a people from Southwest Asia, who settled in the Nile delta from 1750 BC.

The New Kingdom (Eighteenth to Twentieth dynasties inclusive)

The Hyksös were finally driven out of Egypt by Pharaoh Ahmose, and a new capital was established at Thebes. Under the successors of Ahmose, Egyptian civilisation reached its zenith, with grand temples being built throughout the Nile valley and the kingdom expanding eastwards, into Asia, as far as the river Euphrates. Pharaoh Akhenaton tried, but failed, to reform Egypt's religion. In Asia, Egyptian lands were attacked by the Hittites, and for many years Pharaoh Rameses II, 'the Great', fought a long and bitter war against them. Although Rameses III defeated an invasion by the Indo-European 'peoples of the sea', the power of Egypt began to decline, and effective authority passed from the pharaohs to the priests of Amun during the latter part of the Twentieth Dynasty.

The Third Intermediate period
(Twenty-first to Twenty-third dynasties inclusive)

During the Twenty-first Dynasty, rival pharaohs based themselves at Thebes and Tanis, until Egypt was eventually reunified under Pharaoh Psusennes II. A Libyan family seized power when he died in 945 BC, instigating one-hundred-and-fifty years of violent struggle between the priests of Amun and rival Libyan chieftains.

The Late period (Twenty-fourth to Thirty-first dynasties inclusive)

The Nubian kingdom of the Kushites reunited Egypt, which was then invaded by Assyria, whose troops occupied Thebes. Egypt had regained its independence by the time of the Twenty-sixth Dynasty, only to be occupied by Persia. These ancient empires wanted possession of the fertile Nile delta, known as the 'breadbasket of the Mediterranean', and foreign cultures began to overlay the distinctive Egyptian civilisation. Nectanebos II was the last native-born pharaoh, and he was eventually driven out by the Persians. Egypt was eventually conquered by Alexander the Great of Macedon, who created a new capital at Alexandria. Ptolemy, Alexander's general, founded the Macedonian, or Ptolemaic, Dynasty, which ended with the death of Cleopatra, after which Egypt became a province of the Roman Empire.

Index

Bibliography

Mysteries and Secrets of Magic, C.J.S. Thompson, Senate 1995

Egyptian Life, Miriam Stead, British Museum Press 1994

The New Larousse Encyclopaedia of Mythology, Ed. Felix Guirand, Hamlyn 1975

The Keys of Egypt, Lesley & Roy Adkins, Harper Collins 2000

The Book of Divination, Christine Smith, Rider 1978

Tales of Ancient Egypt, Roger Lancelyn Green, Puffin 1970

Egyptian Birth Signs, Storm Constantine Thorsons 2002